Bigger Faster Stronger

Greg Shepard, EdD

Human Kinetics

Library of Congress Cataloging-in-Publication Data

Shepard, Greg, 1942-
  Bigger faster stronger / Greg Shepard.
     p. cm.
Includes bibliographical references and index.
  ISBN 0-7360-4814-6 (softcover)
  1. High school athletes--Training of. 2. School sports. 3. Physical
education and training--Study and teaching (Secondary) I. Title.
  GV346.S55 2003
  613.7'11--dc21

                                                                2003004604

ISBN: 0-7360-4814-6

The Web addresses cited in this text were current as of April 9, 2003, unless otherwise noted.

Acquisitions Editor: Ed McNeely; **Managing Editor:** Wendy McLaughlin; **Assistant Editor:** Kim Thoren; **Copyeditor:** Bob Replinger; **Proofreader:** Susan C. Hagan; **Indexer:** Betty Frizzéll; **Permission Manager:** Toni Harte; **Graphic Designer:** Nancy Rasmus; **Graphic Artist:** Tara Welsch; **Art and Photo Manager:** Dan Wendt; **Cover Designer:** Keith Blomberg; **Illustrator:** Bigger Faster Stronger™; **Printer:** United Graphics

Human Kinetics books are available at special discounts for bulk purchase. Special editions or book excerpts can also be created to specification. For details, contact the Special Sales Manager at Human Kinetics.

Printed in the United States of America   10   9   8   7   6   5   4   3   2   1

Human Kinetics
Web site: www.HumanKinetics.com

United States: Human Kinetics, P.O. Box 5076, Champaign, IL 61825-5076
800-747-4457
e-mail: humank@hkusa.com

Canada: Human Kinetics, 475 Devonshire Road Unit 100, Windsor, ON N8Y 2L5
800-465-7301 (in Canada only)
e-mail: orders@hkcanada.com

Europe: Human Kinetics, 107 Bradford Road, Stanningley, Leeds LS28 6AT, United Kingdom
+44 (0) 113 255 5665
e-mail: hk@hkeurope.com

Australia: Human Kinetics, 57A Price Avenue, Lower Mitcham, South Australia 5062
08 8277 1555
e-mail: liaw@hkaustralia.com

New Zealand: Human Kinetics, Division of Sports Distributors NZ Ltd.
P.O. Box 300 226 Albany, North Shore City, Auckland
0064 9 448 1207
e-mail: blairc@hknewz.com

Bigger Faster Stronger

CONTENTS

ACKNOWLEDGMENTS

I would like to acknowledge those individuals who have helped throughout the years in developing my knowledge of strength and conditioning: Dr. Phil Allsen, Dr. Lavon Johnson, Dr. L. Jay Silvester, Dr. Ed Reuter, Don Tollefson, George Frenn, Coach Al Decoria, Coach Herb Langeman, Coach Verl Shell, and Coach Gerald Crittenden. Thanks also to BFS clinicians, Jim Brown, Jeff Scurran, Len Walencikowski, Rick Bojak, Bob Doyle, Doug Ekmark, Dennis Dunn, Bob Bozied, Mandy Eakin, Jeff Sellers, Evan Ayers, Mark Beckham, Doug Holland, Roger Freeborn, Bobby Poss, Ray Cosenza, Rick Tomberlin, Patti Hagemeyer, and Matt Merry.

Special thanks to my Bigger Faster Stronger partners, Rick Anderson and Bob Rowbotham, and the thousands of coaches and athletes who have participated in the Bigger Faster Stronger program and clinics. And to my wife, Diana Shepard, for her proofing of the book.

More than 9,000 high schools have implemented the Bigger Faster Stronger (BFS) program. More than 300 of those schools have won state championships in football after having had BFS clinics. Many college teams and high-profile professional athletes are reaping success with BFS, and each year our clinicians schedule more than 250 seminars. In an independent survey through the University of Minnesota, 40 percent of the high school football coaches polled said that they use BFS as their primary source of strength and conditioning information. Over 250,000 students have gone through a BFS clinic. BFS is not a here-today-gone-tomorrow workout system but a popular and effective training method with a 30-year history of success. What is not widely known is how the program developed. That history is a vital component of the achievements of BFS today. So, where did the program come from?

As I think about the origins of today's BFS program, I can point to three primary sources: George Frenn, the high school and college athletes I coached from the mid-1960s to the late 1970s, and the late Stefan Fernholm. Those athletes provided me with the practical experience to refine the BFS system so that it could be easily taught and implemented in the United States.

George Frenn was one of the best hammer throwers in the country with a best competitive squat of 843 pounds—long before the days of super suits and other special supportive equipment. He was so far ahead of everyone else that it was obvious there was something different about his training. I wanted to know his secrets! So, in the late 1960s, I spent my summers in the Los Angeles area to be near George and pick his brain.

Also joining George were elite throwers from all over the country who came to live in the Los Angeles area, where they could throw year round with many of the best athletes in the world. As a football coach, I looked with amazement at the conditioning of those guys. At least 30 were in the group, and they weighed an average of 270 pounds and ran 4.6 to 4.7 seconds in the 40-yard dash. They were far bigger, faster, and stronger than the pro football players of that era. I wanted those types of athletes on my football team.

What was their secret? It was simple, but radical at the time. They stretched, lifted hard with free weights, varied their workouts, and concentrated on the big multijoint lifts that develop the legs and hips. They added sprint and jump training.

Their success told me that all athletes, regardless of their sport, should focus their strength training on the squat and power clean. Those lifts may be augmented by doing a few, but only a few, auxiliary lifts. And athletes should complement the lifting and stretching with speed drills and plyometric jump drills. Those were simple ideas, but the best.

I took what I learned from George back to my high school. In 1970 I was a coach at Sehome High School in Bellingham, Washington. Sehome's enrollment of 1,400 nudged us into the big-school category, but we were among the smallest in our classification. Despite our size, we won the unofficial state championship against a school with almost twice our enrollment. Our athletes were simply too good. The opposing team produced minus 77 yards in that championship game! I also coached track, and 11 of our guys could throw the discus between 140 and 180 feet. If an athlete couldn't throw 155 feet, he was a JV guy. To this day I don't believe any high school has ever been able to say that. We had a bunch of kids who could bench 300, squat 400, and power clean 250 pounds—lifts that college athletes would be proud of.

My next challenge was as head football coach at a high school in Idaho. I inherited a team that was 0-6 and had lost homecoming 72-0. The kids were so dispirited that they just quit, forfeiting their last three games. We trained hard, and the following year our team won the county championships and scored a fantastic 29-16 victory over the team that had beat us 72-0, despite the fact that the opposing team had a school enrollment of 1,600 kids to our 850. Then I took over the Granger High School team in Salt Lake City, a team that had won only two ballgames in four years. We achieved what is still considered the most dramatic turnaround in the history of Utah, and as a result I received the Utah football coach of the year award.

Coaches were asking me, "How can you take a disaster school and turn it around in just one year?" When I said we did it with our weight-training program, they asked me to come to their schools and show them how to do it. That was how our BFS clinics began, and the schools that I worked with turned around their programs.

In between my football jobs at Washington and Idaho, I was hired as the strength coach at Brigham Young University. At BYU I did a movie called *Bigger Faster Stronger*. The movie was a hit, and the secret was out nationwide. Football coaches nationwide began using the BFS progam, but even so, it seemed to be a slow process. It was also amazing to me that coaches from other sports just could not get it.

The NBA did not start hiring strength coaches until the 1980s, and with pro baseball it took until the 1990s. Even today, among high school athletes in all boys' and girls' sports, less than half possess the secret to becoming bigger, faster, and stronger. It is simple—if athletes want to be successful and unlock their full potential, they must use the secret.

The third major contributor to our BFS program was Stefan Fernholm, a discus thrower from Sweden who came to BYU to compete at the college level. He broke the NCAA collegiate record and was a past Olympian. Stefan became a part of BFS in the mid-1980s. We owe him a great deal. He bridged the gap between the United States and the old Soviet Union. Stefan was privy to and knowledgeable about Soviet training methods.

Stefan taught all our clinicians, including me, the value of perfecting technique. Perfection became our focus. Athletes must know all the secrets, but they must also be able to execute every facet perfectly to put it all together.

With solid research, over 40 years of practical knowledge, and tens of thousands of athletes using the program, we've got it right. The BFS program is the perfect program for any high school athlete, male or female, and it's ideal for coaches who deal with large numbers of athletes. The program has also shown remarkable success at the college level. Why not join the BFS team and make memories you'll be proud to share?

PART I

The Total Program

A Unified Approach to Training

All high school and most college athletes should perform the same basic strength and conditioning program, and all coaches should teach the same training philosophy—regardless of the sport. Such organization reduces teaching time, prevents many administrative hassles and personality conflicts, and improves athletic performance. I call this philosophy *unification*.

One of the worst problems for the multisport athlete is having each coach prescribe a unique strength and conditioning program. I've visited many high schools where the football coach did an intense program primarily with free weights and the girls' basketball coach did little strength training and used only machines. The girls' coach would say, "My girls are intimidated by free weights," and would limit their strength training to inferior exercises on a multistation machine. The boys' baseball coach would tell the players, "Hey, weights will make you muscle bound," and would have them do no strength training whatsoever.

A high school may have as many as seven different strength-training programs! The same goes for each broad area of training: speed, warm-up, endurance, agility, plyometrics, and flexibility. Even not addressing some of the preceding areas in a conditioning program is a coaching philosophy. For example, the baseball coach who does not make strength training an integral part of the in-season program and never works with the athletes on how to run faster sends a message to the players.

Territorial struggles between coaches unnecessarily test the loyalty of the athlete. The result is that the coaches often force athletes to participate in only one sport, which adversely affects the overall quality of the school's athletic program. The unnecessary tension between coaching staffs is often the rule rather than the exception for high schools and small colleges.

If coaches adopt the Bigger Faster Stronger system, all athletes perform the same basic program throughout the entire school year and during the summer. Confusion disappears, coaches enjoy a spirit of teamwork with their colleagues, and athletes more easily achieve their goals. That's why it's no surprise to us when a school's athletic program does an immediate turnaround after we've set up a unified program at a BFS clinic.

All athletes can benefit from the BFS speed, strength, and jump program.

ELEMENTARY AND HIGH SCHOOL PROGRAMS

At BFS clinics we go beyond simply teaching reps, sets, and exercises. Our clinicians teach coaches and administrators how to unify their athletic program so that it encompasses all sports, for both male and female athletes, from grades 7 through 12. And to keep the terminology simple, we give the school the option of calling it the BFS total program or naming it after their school mascot. Let's say a school's teams are the Wildcats. Everyone does the Wildcats stretching program. The Wildcats would also have a unified speed, warm-up, endurance, agility, plyometrics, and weight-training program. It's that simple—and it works!

With unification, a two- or three-sport Wildcats athlete would move smoothly from sport season to sport season without interruption. Let's take the example of a football player who is also on the basketball team. After the football season, this athlete would not have to wait four to six weeks to get started on some unique basketball-specific strength-training program. He would just stay on the Wildcats in-season program. Athletes don't have the Wildcats *basketball* in-season program, they just have the Wildcats in-season program. This approach makes the coach's job easier because he or she doesn't have to waste time teaching several new or different lifting exercises. Also, the same warm-up (for example, BFS dot drill) and flexibility exercises just naturally continue. It's what all Wildcats do!

Junior high school athletes would follow the same guidelines. After they learn proper technique, seventh graders can do the same workouts that high school athletes do. In fact, because the level of competition at the high school level continues to reach higher standards, athletes must get into the weight room as soon as possible so that they don't fall behind. Just think of the advantages when those young kids, who are maturing and developing on the Wildcats total program, get to high school!

Bob Giesey is a coach at American Heritage Academy in Carrollton, Texas. Since 1985 he has started his athletes on the BFS program as early as the third grade (a group he calls the ankle biters). Here are 20 benefits he came up with about getting elementary-age athletes involved in BFS:

1. Develops competitive spirit through physical drills
2. Provides excellent physical conditioning
3. Develops a working attitude

Young women who train hard with the BFS unified approach dominate their competition in every sport.

4. Teaches discipline that will positively affect their daily living and academics
5. Builds teamwork
6. Develops personalities
7. Increases confidence
8. Creates a sense of belonging to a group
9. Improves communication, which in turn improves trust
10. Teaches responsibility, which in turn improves caring for others and equipment
11. Allows them to see how hard others are working to reach objectives
12. Teaches respect
13. Develops enthusiasm individually and as a group
14. Teaches athletes to dream to achieve
15. Teaches the value of commitment
16. Helps them to be organized (dress, equipment, and so on)
17. Develops good decision-making skills
18. Teaches promptness
19. Promotes participation in middle school and high school sports
20. Permits an easy transition from grade school to middle school to high school

COLLEGE PROGRAMS

Many Division I schools have outstanding sport-conditioning programs, and every month we profile the best college programs in our magazine. But it would be presumptuous for me to suggest that the BFS program is better than the program at Oklahoma or Miami or any other Division I school. I will say, however, that most Division II, Division III, NAIA (National Association of Intercollegiate Athletics), and junior college programs would be successful with the total BFS program simply because it more fully addresses those particular situations and athletes. The BFS program is also easy for coaches to implement, which is especially important for small colleges that do not have full-time strength coaches to develop specific programs for each sport.

What if a Division I athlete misses a workout? He or she might lose a scholarship. What about the high school athlete? The BFS program is designed to create massive voluntary participation with daily increases of self-confidence; the athletes want to train hard and not miss workouts. The BFS system also flows easily from one sport to the next and unifies all sports into an easily managed total strength and conditioning program.

One example of the effectiveness of unification is the program that Roger VanDeZande ran at Southern Oregon University. VanDeZande, who was also the defensive coordinator, was solely responsible for supervising the conditioning programs of more than 250 athletes in numerous sports. VanDeZande used the BFS program at the high school level and knew that he would be working with a large number of athletes when he went to SOU. He saw no reason to change his coaching philosophy. "When I look at many of the teams we've hammered despite their superior talent and facilities, it's obvious that if they were doing what they should be doing they would beat us," says VanDeZande.

UNIFICATION MANAGEMENT

Although more than one million athletes have used the BFS program, less than 2 percent of all high schools in America have adopted a true unified program. This means that over 17,000 high schools do not implement their strength and conditioning program correctly. Unification offers many advantages over other programs, and it's why coaches from all sports enthusiastically accept our presentations at BFS clinics.

Although I will cover equipment considerations later in this book, I strongly recommend using two products to build a quality, unified program that will help all athletes, both male and female, in all sports. First is a lightweight Olympic barbell such as the BFS Aluma-Lite, which weighs 15 pounds, along with 5- and 10-pound Olympic-size training plates. Teaching important Olympic lifting exercises is much easier with this equipment, because the barbell with weights can weigh as little as 25 pounds. Athletes can concentrate on technique because they won't worry about the weight or be forced to bend too low with smaller-sized plates.

Next is some type of detailed record keeping in the form of personal logbooks or a computer spreadsheet program. Keeping records helps athletes set daily goals, and they receive positive reinforcement when they see their long-term progress in print.

Logbooks work well in any situation. For larger programs, a quality software program is a way to keep track of literally hundreds of athletes. John Hoch is the head football coach at Lancaster High School in Lancaster, Wisconsin. After the Lancaster football team compiled a 41-1 record in three years, Coach Hoch's story appeared in *BFS* magazine. In that interview he praised our computer system, which is called Beat the Computer. "Beat the Computer has made my job unbelievably easier," said Hoch. "You can print out the program by specific sports, which is really great because more and more of our kids are getting involved with weights."

Coach Hoch also found that our computer program helped motivate his athletes to train harder: "Our kids are always pushing themselves on their final sets, but the Beat the Computer program pushed them on their first and second sets—or if it's a long program, on the first through the fourth sets. This made the final set really a challenge. It really made a difference in getting our athletes strong."

The BFS program combines the best of strength and conditioning from all over the world. The system recognizes the great differences between elite, pro, and college athletes compared with those at the high school level. The BFS program is perfect for large numbers of athletes, block schedules, females, junior high schools, in-season and off-season transitions, and the multisport athlete, and it creates great self-confidence and massive voluntary participation.

Unification: It just makes sense!

Smyrna Eagles—Flying High

Located in a rural community surrounded by farmland, Smyrna High School in Smyrna, Delaware, has only about 900 students. Until recently, athletes from this school usually didn't attract much attention outside the city limits. But through hard work, community support and the recent addition of the BFS Total Program, the Smyrna High School Eagles are making their presence felt throughout the entire state.

In 2002 the girls' basketball team not only had a great regular season, but they also made it to the second round in the state tournament for the first time in the school's history. Not to be outdone, the boys' basketball team also competed in the state tournament for the first time since 1993. The girls' field hockey team advanced to the second round of the state tournament for the first time in a decade, and the boys' baseball team reached the state tournament for the first time in five years.

Although there are many factors contributing to the recent success of Smyrna High School athletes, head wrestling coach and physical education teacher Clay Lloyd believes that much of the improvement can be attributed to adopting the BFS program in 2000. "The overall attitude, work ethic, and con-

After committing to the BFS program, the women's field hockey team at Smyrna High became serious contenders for the state championships.

fidence level of our athletes have improved across the board, and I believe this is a direct reflection of instituting the BFS program."

Lloyd, who in 2002 coached his grapplers to a second place finish in the state tournament for teams (Division II), began the conversion to BFS by implementing the program in his regular weight-training class. This class was attended by regular and special education students and a few athletes. It quickly became one of the school's most popular classes. "The class was so successful that I took it to the athletic director, and he agreed with me that the BFS program should be available to all our athletes." Now Lloyd says that at least one in four students at Smyrna is on the BFS program. And the participation continues to grow.

When Lloyd first converted his athletes to BFS, he started with the BFS workout cards. Soon he switched to the Beat the Computer program. "The workout cards are great, but the Beat the Computer program dramatically reduced the amount of time I had to spend with record keeping," says Lloyd. "Before the BFS Beat the Computer program, my athletes and weight training class students occupied much of my time with questions such as 'How much should I start with?' and 'How much should I lift on my next set?' The computer program answers those questions, and it's easy to adjust if the weights were too light or too heavy. These advantages saved a lot of time and allowed me to focus on other aspects of coaching."

In addition to enthusiastically following the BFS workout, the Eagles have also embraced the BFS Be An Eleven program. "We take lessons and messages from the *Be An Eleven Guidebook for Success* and try to instill those ideals within our athletes."

Lloyd says he is expecting great things from the athletes who will be on the BFS program throughout their entire high school terms. Indeed, the Smyrna Eagles have already transformed themselves into state-caliber competitors ready to soar high.

BFS Rotational Set-Rep System

Many workout programs fail because their exercise prescriptions are so monotonous that the body adapts to them and is therefore no longer stimulated to make progress. But this is not the case with the BFS rotational set-rep system, a proven training program that rotates the weekly set-rep prescriptions so that athletes can set records on a daily basis.

As an athlete, you will always be in a position to make continual progress with the BFS program. No other program can do this. If you have been doing three sets of 10 reps, one set of 15, and five sets of 5, you no doubt reach a plateau very quickly. You cannot do the same workout time after time without paying this price. Instead, you must alternate all the variables: lifts, percentage of maximums, sets, and reps. Systems that are more complex, such as cycling regimens, are better than some workouts for delivering steady progress, but you will still eventually hit a plateau. The BFS system allows you to alternate your lifts, sets, and reps in such a way that you repeat a specific workout only every fifth week. This system has two simple rules: First, establish your records and second, break those records. If you follow this system exactly, you will never reach a plateau.

Being able to break records frequently is extremely motivating, especially for a young athlete. Although older athletes may be satisfied with breaking a personal record for a lift once a month, younger athletes are often impatient and quickly lose interest in such a program.

Two more important advantages of the BFS rotational set-rep system are that it is simple to use and can be implemented easily with a large number of athletes. Such versatility makes the BFS program perfect for high schools and small colleges, most of which do not have the financial and personnel resources of Division I college programs.

Countless athletes at thousands of high schools have used the BFS rotational set-rep system over the past 26 years. Andy Griffin, a highly successful Texas high school football coach, gave us a typical response after implementing the program: "When is this going to stop? I mean, can they keep breaking records like this? My athletes have broken so many records these past months, I can't believe it. Thanks!" Yes, they will. I guarantee eight new personal records per week for as long as the athletes are in high school.

OVERCOMING PLATEAUS

In weight training, everyone experiences plateaus, a leveling off or even a dropping off in performance. People can become frustrated, depressed, and ready to quit because of this phenomenon. A leveling off of performance happens to everyone, but there are ways to prolong upward movement and overcome plateaus.

I'll share with you a ridiculous example to make a point. A coach says, "Men, we are going to improve our 40-yard dash. We are going to sprint 40-yard dashes 20 times every day, and I guarantee you will become faster." All the athletes are psyched, and they do it. Afterward each athlete says, "I'm really tired, but this is going to be good for us. Thanks, Coach." No problem so far, right? Well, what would happen if the athletes had to do the same sprint workout five days a week for eight weeks? Obviously, by the eighth week the kids would hate it, and the times for the 40-yard dash probably would have become worse. The athletes would have gone through what is known as Hans Selye's stress syndrome. For some it might take three days, for others, weeks. But everyone will go through it.

Hans Selye defined his stress syndrome in 1928 to explain why some individuals become sick while others remain healthy when being exposed to the same viruses and bacteria. He found that when a person is subjected to any kind of stress, he or she will go through all or part of this syndrome. I have adapted his theory to the BFS rotational set-rep system. The idea makes sense, and it works.

For example, a person goes outside and is ready to jump into an unheated pool. His friends say, "Come on in. The water's fine once you get used to it." So he jumps in. First he is in shock and wants to choke his friends, but then he starts to get used to it. That's countershock. Soon he is jumping in and out and having a great time. This is the stage of resistance. Eventually, in a matter of hours, depending on the temperature of the water, he will start to freeze and will even die if he stays in. This final stage, exhaustion, usually happens quickly. In two-a-days, for example, most athletes reach the stage of resistance by the fifth or sixth day. The problem is how to prolong the stage of resistance throughout the entire season and not enter the stage of exhaustion. See figure 2.1.

Selye's stress theory can easily be applied to sets and reps in weight training. If an athlete does three sets of 10 every day with the same exercises, the stage of exhaustion will rear its ugly head in about four weeks. The same would be true of one set of 8 to 12 reps or five sets of 5 reps.

The trick is to vary the sets, reps, exercises, and intensity as much as possible. Every time a variation is inserted into the program, the stage of resistance will be prolonged. The BFS rotational set-rep system offers a great deal of variation. Every day is different. A given workout occurs only every fifth week. The system of breaking records is highly motivational, which helps prolong the stage of resistance. Here are seven other ways to prolong resistance:

- Use charts for motivation and design them so that everyone feels successful.

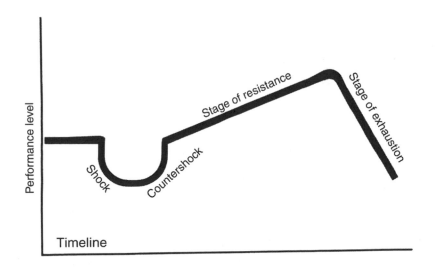

Figure 2.1 Hans Selye's stress theory.

■ Periodically set dates for competitions against other individuals or schools, or for a new maximum.

■ Use motivational films, stories, and people periodically.

■ Use awards (shirts, certificates, and so on).

■ Vary the time, place, days, partners, sequence, intensity, or diet.

■ Increase diet, sleep, or rest.

■ When athletes return after a layoff, have them forget all past achievements and start an all-new set of records.

Note that simply having a regular but varied routine is itself an important way to prolong the stage of resistance. The challenge for coaches is to find an optimum balance between regularity of routine and appropriate variations that will enable their athletes to make constant progress and avoid plateaus. The system can break down when athletes enter a plateau or the stage of exhaustion, because the traditional response is to work harder and increase the intensity of the workout. This approach usually makes things worse. More rest, not more work, is most likely what the athletes need. Overcoming plateaus and combating stress are as much an art as a science. A coach should be sensitive in this area. By developing expertise in prolonging the stage of resistance, the coach will undoubtedly prolong his or her coaching tenure.

USING PERIODIZATION OR BFS?

The BFS rotational set-rep system is superior to both the most sophisticated periodization system and the so-called Russian and Bulgarian systems. The BFS system flows perfectly from one sport season to the next and is perfect for a team-concept approach. High school athletes will make more progress with greater winning intensity and will be more motivated than they will with any other system available worldwide. These are bold statements, so let's analyze why they are true.

Periodization is dividing an annual plan of training into phases to attain peaks during the most important competitions. Some people categorize these phases as preparation, competition, and transition. These phases are normally broken down into subphases called macro- or microcycles. Each cycle varies the sets, reps, exercises, percentages, and training intensity (that is, the amount of weight lifted).

We know that Eastern European coaches tend to use advanced forms of periodization, but because they use many variations we cannot identify a specific system. Stefan Fernholm, a former BFS staff member who was an elite Swedish athlete and familiar with those systems, remembers hearing Russians snicker at the foolish Americans who thought they understood how to train like Russians. We have mountains of research you could wade through from Russian and Eastern European compendiums. My advice is to let your competition use a Bulgarian weightlifter's routine for a high school football team.

On the surface, the periodization cycles used by elite athletes in the Eastern Bloc countries seem to have great merit. Many top universities espouse periodization. So why shouldn't high schools do the same? Here are five reasons:

1. **Training teams.** Periodization was originally intended for individuals. Many universities train their athletes in small groups. Individual workouts are put on a computer printout. High schools have an advantage. They can work out as a team. Coaches can organize the workout as they would a practice. With the BFS system, the intensity levels of teams and individuals can reach incredible heights. Periodization systems are much more sporadic when it comes to intensity.

2. **Peaking is a major problem.** When do you peak? Do you choose to peak for homecoming, the conference championship, or the playoffs? In Bulgaria, you would peak for one major contest each year. In American football, you had better have some sort of peak every week, or you won't have to worry about peaking for the playoffs.

3. **Training the multisport athlete.** Universities and Eastern Europeans normally deal only with one-sport athletes. A periodization program done halfway properly in a high school could drive a coach nuts with its complexities. For example, after the football season 15 of the 65 players go into basketball, 20 go out for wrestling, and the remaining 30 kids are in an off-season program. Then in March, 12 of the football players who play basketball go out for a spring sport—7 go out for baseball, and 5 go out for track. The other 3 basketball-football players join the off-season program. The 30 kids who were in the off-season program now split into different groups. Twenty have decided to enter a spring sport. In the summer, 17 football players also play baseball, while others attend basketball, wrestling, and football camps. Wow! Did you get all that? Athletes would be running in and out of phases and cycles all year long, requiring many different schedules and programs. Administering a periodization program for a large group of high school athletes would be a nightmare.

Wouldn't it be smart to have a periodization or cycle program that adapted beautifully to all those situations so that the transitions from one sport season to the next required no extra work by the coach? Wouldn't it be great to see your athletes continually progress throughout every in-season and reach their fullest potential with superior team intensity? That scenario describes our BFS rotational set-rep system.

4. Obtaining accurate maxes. An athlete has a 175-pound clean, and he's supposed to train with 60 percent at 105 pounds, 70 percent at 122.5 pounds, 80 percent at 140 pounds, and so on. Yet after I go to a clinic and teach that athlete about intensity and technique, he will typically clean 225 pounds. So now what? In all probability, much of his training with 110 and 130 pounds during an eight-week periodization cycle was unproductive.

5. Progress is too slow. The BFS rotational set-rep system provides intensity-filled, challenging and motivating training sessions. Computer printouts don't allow for daily variance in strength. The BFS system corrects itself on a set basis during the workout. The athlete doesn't have to wait for long periods to break a record. On the BFS system he or she breaks records every workout. Periodization can hold high school teams back, whereas our BFS system propels teams forward week after week at breakneck speed.

It's true that we've borrowed selectively from periodization and Russian-European systems. We've packaged the most appropriate training practices into a system that works amazingly well for high school athletes involved in team sports, while taking into consideration their unique time and logistics constraints. Let your competition try to sort out all the research and come up with a periodization program. Let your competition copy the system of a Russian weightlifter. Let your competition use the university's program and scramble to adapt it to the high school situation. Meanwhile, with the progressive and reliable BFS system, you'll be getting all the results you've been looking for.

THE WORKOUT

The BFS system for off-season training is set up on four-week cycles, with each week consisting of the following core lifts performed on specific days. Although the order of the lifts remains the same, each week you will use a different set-rep prescription for the core lifts. Table 2.1 illustrates this four-week cycle. See table 2.2 for a real-life example.

Record keeping is especially important with the BFS rotational set-rep system because you often break records every training day, making it easy to lose track of your progress without some type of logbook. How do you know if you are improving if you don't mark down what you've done in the past? Many coaches use teachers' aides to assist the athletes

Table 2.1　BFS Total Program

Monday	Tueday	Wednesday	Thursday	Friday
Squat variation	Sprint work	Power clean	Sprint work	Parallel squat
Bench variation	Plyometrics	Hex bar	Plyometrics	Bench press
Auxiliary lifts	Flexibility	Auxiliary lifts	Flexibility	Auxiliary lifts
Flexibility	Agility	Flexibility	Agility	Flexibility
Agility	Technique	Agility	Technique	Agility

Table 2.2　Four-Week Training Cycle

Week 1	The first week is easy. After warm-ups, do 3 × 3. On the last set, do 3 or more. Give an all-out effort!
Week 2	Do 5 × 5 or, if you have only 45 minutes of class time, cut it down to 3 × 5. Doing 5 × 5 is difficult, even brutal. On the last set, do 5 or more. Again, give your all.
Week 3	Do 5-4-3-2-1 or, if time is a problem, do 5-3-1. This is moderately difficult. On the last set, do 1 or more.
Week 4	Establish another set record and records for more reps. Do 10-8-6 on the bench, towel bench, squat, and box squat, and do 4-4-2 on the clean and deadlift or hex-bar lift. *Important concept:* Do 6 or more reps or 2 or more reps on the last set, depending on the core lift.
Week 5	Start the rotation over with the workout for week 1. Do more weight than in week 1 and break more set and rep records.

The reps and sets outlined above *do not* include warm-up sets and are not necessarily relevant to all core lifts or auxiliary exercises. For example, a set-rep scheme of 4-4-2 (4 reps, 4 reps, 2 reps) is prescribed on week 4 for the power clean and the hex-bar deadlift because it's difficult to maintain perfect form on those exercises with higher reps.

with record keeping. See the appendix for more log book entries. The complete logbook can be obtained by contacting BFS.

Now let's carefully go through the core lifts and set-rep schemes for an entire training cycle, starting with week 1, Monday.

Monday, Week 1 (3 × 3)

This first workout may seem too easy, but keep in mind that the main concern here is making sure that you follow the proper spotting and lifting techniques.

■ **Box squats.** On the first set select between 45 and 145 pounds for 3 reps. For the second set, you may either go up in poundage, stay the same, or go down. For example, if you feel good about 145, you can go up to 175 pounds on your second set and then 205 for the third set. On the final set, you should do 3 or more reps, up to 10 reps if you can.

■ **Towel bench.** If you, like most athletes, know your max on the bench, take 70 percent of your max for your first set. For example, if your max is 200 pounds, begin with 140 pounds for 3 reps on your first set. If you've never done benches before, use 70 percent of your body weight or 105 pounds, whichever is less. If this is too much weight for 3 reps, use 60 percent or even 50 percent of your body weight. For your second set, you may go up, stay the same, or go down. Do 3 or more reps on the final set but on this first workout select a weight that you can do 10 times. If possible, you want to establish your rep records for all lifts you will record.

■ **Record keeping.** Now it's time to record your records. Say your results were as follows:

Box squat: 145 + 175 + 205 = 525

Towel bench: 140 + 150 + 150 = 440

■ **Establish set and rep records.** The total amount of weight lifted is your set record. In the example, the box-squat set record is 525 pounds and the towel-bench set record is 440 pounds. In the sample training log in figure 2.2, notice the box labeled actual reps. This is where you will record the reps you made on your last set.

For your rep record, follow this example. Let's say you did 10 reps at 205 on the box squat and 10 reps at 150 on the towel bench on the final set. Record your box-squat and towel-bench rep records. Simply write in the weight lifted for the correct number of reps and write the date in the box at the upper right (figure 2.3). Figure 2.4 is an example of how to record your success for the towel bench.

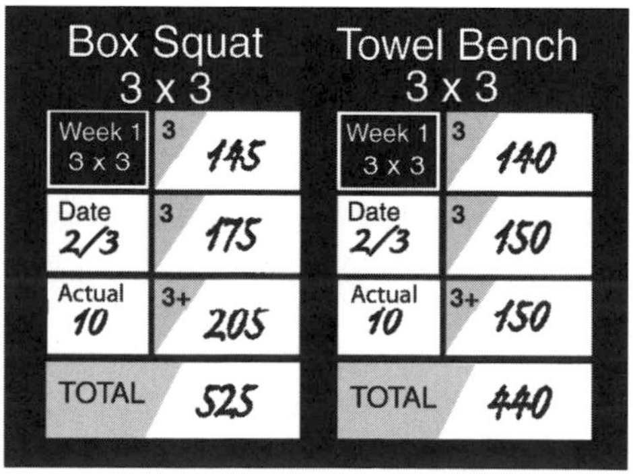

Box Squat 3 x 3		Towel Bench 3 x 3	
Week 1 3 x 3	3 *145*	Week 1 3 x 3	3 *140*
Date 2/3	3 *175*	Date 2/3	3 *150*
Actual 10	3+ *205*	Actual 10	3+ *150*
TOTAL	*525*	TOTAL	*440*

Figure 2.2 This is an example of establishing set records.

BOX SQUAT			TOWEL BENCH		
REP	Establish Records		**REP**	Establish Records	
1	Date 2/3	Weight 205	1	Date 2/3	Weight 150
2	Date 2/3	Weight 205	2	Date 2/3	Weight 150
3	Date 2/3	Weight 205	3	Date 2/3	Weight 150
4	Date 2/3	Weight 205	4	Date 2/3	Weight 150
5	Date 2/3	Weight 205	5	Date 2/3	Weight 150
6	Date 2/3	Weight 205	6	Date 2/3	Weight 150
8	Date 2/3	Weight 205	8	Date 2/3	Weight 150
10	Date 2/3	Weight 205	10	Date 2/3	Weight 150

Figure 2.3 This is an example of establishing rep records.

EXAMPLE OF RECORDING THE

TOWEL BENCH

Set Records for the 5 x 5 & the 5-4-3-2-1

Week 2 5 x 5		Week 3 5-4-3-2-1	
Week 2 5 x 5	5 145	Week 3 5-4-3-2-1	5 165
Date 2/10	5 150	Date 2/17	4 170
Body weight	5 155	Body weight	3 175
166	5 160	167	2 180
Actual 6	5+ 155	Actual 3	1+ 185
TOTAL	765	TOTAL	875

This athlete did 6 reps on the last set

Record your bodyweight. As you get bigger, you will get stronger.

Figure 2.4 This is an example of recording the towel bench.

Figure 2.5 This is an example of recording rep records.

Wednesday, Week 1 (3 × 3)

■ **Clean.** Do the 3 × 3 workout. Use 70 percent of your maximum. If you've never cleaned before, use 70 percent of your body weight or 105 pounds, whichever is less. Use the same procedure for the second and third sets (as in Monday's workout) and record your efforts. On the final set, you should do 3 or more reps, up to 5 reps. Try to do 5 reps.

■ **Hex-bar deadlift.** Do the 3 × 3 workout. Start with 145 pounds or your body weight, whichever is less. Follow the same procedure and record your efforts. Again, on the final set, you should do 3 or more reps, up to 5 reps.

Friday, Week 1 (3 × 3)

Bench press and squat. Do the 3 × 3 workout. Use the poundage and procedures that you used in Monday's towel-bench and box-squat workouts.

Week 2 (5 × 5)

Do 5 sets of 5 reps (5 × 5). This is a long, brutal workout. You may wish to cut it down to 3 sets of 5 because of time or your energy level, especially on the hex-bar and clean day. Select your poundage as you did in the first week. Record your efforts. You should do 5 or more reps on the last set except when doing the clean or hex bar.

Week 3 (5-4-3-2-1)

Do 5-4-3-2-1. This workout is not quite as hard as 5 × 5, but you may want to cut it down to 5-3-1 because of time constraints or your energy level. In figure 2.5, 165 was lifted for 5 reps, 170 for 4 reps, 185 for 3 reps, and so on. Record your efforts. You will establish your 5-4-3-2-1 set records, and you should be breaking some rep records as illustrated. Do 1 or more reps on the last set.

The third week is a perfect time to max out on a one-rep max just by following the regular routine. Or, once every 3 months you could go 5-3-1 to prevent fatigue at the last set. Another option is to take 10 to 20 pounds off of your 5-4-3-2 rep maxes and then do several singles on the way to a long one-rep max.

Week 4 (10-8-6 or 4-4-2)

Do 10-8-6. You will notice that the rep records go to only 5 reps on the clean and the hex bar or deadlift. Doing extra reps on those two lifts could cause an injury, especially to the lower back. As fatigue sets in, you increase your chances of incurring muscle spasms and failing to maintain correct lifting technique.

Week 5, Starting Over (3 × 3)

Now the fun of the BFS system really begins. From now on, every time you come into the weight room, you have a challenge and an objective. You should try to break as many set and rep records as possible. You begin week 5 by again doing the 3 × 3 workout. You will notice in the previous month's example that the athlete achieved a total of 440 on the towel bench (figure 2.2, page 18). The objective is simply to do more!

Look what happened in the example of the fifth week (3 × 3) for the towel bench—five new records! The athlete smashed the set record (total) by 100 pounds, going from 440 total pounds to 540 pounds. In addition, four new rep records were attained (3 standard reps plus 1 extra rep). Refer to the rep record chart example. Under the third break column, 190 pounds should be recorded along with the date for the 3 × 3. Many athletes like to try to break their 10-rep record after doing 3 × 3, because this is an easy week. We call this a burnout set.

Weeks 6, 7, and 8 (5 × 5, 5-4-3-2-1, then 10-8-6 or 4-4-2)

Break as many rep records as you can! On week 6 break your 5 × 5 set record, on week 7 break your 5-4-3-2-1 set record, and on week 8 break your 10-8-6 set record. If you are trying for a new 6-rep max on week 8 and still have power to spare when you get to the 6th rep, don't stop. Squeeze out as many reps as you can (up to 10). The same goes for the clean and hex bar with the 4-4-2. If you are going for a new 2-rep max and still have power for more reps, do it! Be intense. Remember, each additional rep is a new record. Want to win? Break a record.

Now keep rotating your workouts in the four-week cycle. You can expect to break 8 or more records per week or 400 per year for as long as you want. Each of the six core lifts has 4 set records (3 × 3, 5 × 5 and 5-4-3-2-1), so that's 24 possible set records. The bench press, towel bench, squat, and box squat each have 8 rep records, and the hex bar or deadlift and the clean each have 5 rep records. That's 42 possible rep records, or a total of 60 possible records. When you count the auxiliary lifts and performance tests, you have even more records. That's why it is easy to break so many records. Remember, we are not concerned with breaking only a 1-rep max; we want to break all kinds of rep records. We know, for example, that if we break a 3-rep record, our max will also go up soon.

Helpful Hints

1. "Or more" means the number of reps up to 10 on the bench, towel bench, squat, and box squat and up to 5 reps on the clean and hex bar.
2. Call attention to athletes breaking records. Dothan High School in Alabama has a bell at each station. When an athlete is going for a record, the bell is rung. This practice really seems to increase the intensity.
3. Many coaches use teachers' aides to assist the athletes with record keeping.
4. Changing the sequence of the lifts can help overcome a plateau (for example, the athlete can do the bench first, not the squat).

FINER POINTS

■ **Warm-ups.** If you can lift over 200 pounds for any exercise, you need to do warm-up sets. You usually perform these warm-up sets for 5 reps, and you don't record them in your set-rep logbook. Table 2.3 is your guideline to warm-ups.

For example:

3 × 3 with 275 pounds (warm up with 195 and 235)

5 × 5 with 330 pounds (warm up with 235 and 295)

5-4-3-2-1 with 450 pounds (warm up with 235, 325, and 415)

Notice that all the rep records are the same at this time. Don't worry about that. The numbers will change rapidly as you break your rep records, which will normally happen every workout.

Table 2.3 Warm-Up Guidelines

Routine	Warm-up
>200 lb	0-1 set
200-295 lb	1-2 sets
300-395 lb	2-3 sets
400-495 lb	3-4 sets
500-595 lb	4-5 sets

■ **Missing a rep.** Sometimes you may miss a rep. For example, you're trying to do 3 × 3 with 275 and on the last set you can only do 2 reps. You have two options: (1) Rest and try again with the same poundage or a lighter weight or (2) penalize yourself 5 pounds per 100 pounds on the bar. For example, in the above situation you're penalized 10 pounds, so add 275 + 275 + 265 for your total. If you're lifting in the 500-pound range, your penalty would be 25 pounds for missing 1 rep and 50 pounds for missing 2 reps. See table 2.4 for penalties.

■ **Adjusting.** The BFS system gives you flexibility in adjusting poundage as you progress through your workout. For example, your 3 × 3 set record is 1,095 pounds. So you do your first set with 370 pounds, and it's easy. For your second set you select 390 pounds, and it's super tough. Therefore, on your third set, you bring it back down to 370 pounds. Your new set record total is 1,130 pounds.

■ **Starting over.** You should start your records over after a layoff of four or more weeks, a major sickness, or a big drop in weight. Also, football players should start over after two-a-days.

■ **Achieving records.** The BFS program includes 75 total records. There are 60 records up for grabs each week on the BFS system, plus

Table 2.4 Penalty Table

Range	Penalty	Range	Penalty
100-195 lb	5 lb	400-495 lb	20 lb
200-295 lb	10 lb	500-595 lb	25 lb
300-395 lb	15 lb	600-695 lb	30 lb

15 more if you count auxiliary exercises and performance records (dot drill, sit and reach, 40- and 20-yard sprints, vertical jump, and standing long jump).

Being able to vary your workouts, record your lifts, and plan how to break your records are advantages built into the BFS program. Breaking records at a phenomenal rate is what makes the BFS program unique. In fact, I guarantee that athletes individually will break at least eight new personal records per week for as long as they are in high school and the same would be true for a less-experienced college athlete. What would happen if you broke eight personal records per week for one year? The idea almost boggles the mind, doesn't it? Plateaus almost cease to exist. The sky is the limit!

BFS In-Season Training

You are now beginning the sport season. What do you do with the weights? If your answer is, "Wait until the off-season," you will inevitably lose the edge your athletes developed in the off-season. You must find time to weight train.

Let's say you have a football player who bench pressed 250 pounds right before he put the pads on in August. If he does no weight training in the next few months, he will be benching 220 by November 1, just when he needs to be the strongest. In contrast, if he did the BFS in-season program, he could be possibly benching 280 pounds. This is not just an opinion. Besides feedback from coaches who can vouch for the effectiveness of in-season training, several peer-reviewed research studies back up our evidence.

A weight-training study published in the prestigious *Medicine and Science in Sports* reported that subjects could retain their strength levels for up to 15 weeks even if they reduced the volume of work (total work) by two-thirds. The catch was that the intensity (heaviest total weight) had to be relatively high to achieve those results. Studies on aerobic conditioning have found the same results, namely that it is much easier to retain conditioning (with short but hard workouts) than it is to regain it after a prolonged layoff of no training.

IN-SEASON PROGRAM

If your team is used to training in the off-season and doesn't train in-season, I guarantee that they'll be mentally down at playoff time because of a perceived weakness. Conversely, if you train in-season, your team will be mentally up for the playoffs and will be physically stronger than many teams who were stronger at the start of the season. What is better: being stronger at the beginning of the season or during the playoffs? The truth is that athletes simply must take the time to weight train. Here are the components of a successful in-season program.

■ **Train twice per week.** During the sport season, one training session a week is not enough volume to make progress, whereas three training sessions a week is too draining. In addition, with the carefully selected exercises in the BFS program, you can work out the day before the game without adversely affecting performance.

■ **Train in the morning.** If possible, train in the morning before school or in a weight-training class before lunch. There are disadvantages to weight training just before or just after practice. You'll get better results by getting up a half hour earlier to lift (a workout many coaches like to call "brawn at dawn") than by trying to lift before or after practice.

■ **Keep it to 30 minutes.** You should keep in-season weight-training workouts to 30 minutes or less. Remember, the objective of training is to win in your sport. You must focus a lot of time and energy on your sport during the season, and you simply cannot afford to spend many hours in the weight room. Two 30-minute sessions for a total of one hour during the week is sufficient, and it's amazing how much progress you can make in that time.

■ **Emphasize the basic BFS core lifts.** You want to have your parallel squat, bench, and clean progressing throughout the season—you just can't let those go. However, you can skip many auxiliary exercises.

The beauty of doing the box squat in-season is that recovery occurs almost immediately. You can box squat heavy on Thursday and still play hard on Friday. To avoid overtraining, male athletes should generally keep the poundage on the box squat within about 100 pounds of the parallel squat. Female athletes should stay within about 75 pounds. Likewise, the towel bench press is an effective in-season exercise, because it keeps the stress level down while allowing you to make some progress on the bench. The towel bench press puts much less stress on the shoulder-joint area than the regular bench press does, an important consideration in contact sports that put a lot of punishment on the shoulders. Therefore, you do this lift on Wednesday or Thursday before the game.

You should perform the straight-leg deadlift with light weights during the season, no more than 30 percent of your parallel-squat max. Most high school athletes will therefore be lifting between 55 and 135 pounds on this exercise for two sets of 10 reps. The primary objectives of the straight-leg deadlift are to get a good hamstring and glute stretch while building strength in that area. Remember, this exercise is crucial to improving speed. You would not plug this exercise into the normal BFS set-rep routine.

■ **Do only three big sets.** Just follow our BFS set-rep system during in-season, as follows:

Former Green Packers football legend Reggie White performed box squats in-season to help him stay strong for every game.

- ■ Week 1: 3 × 3
- ■ Week 2: 3 × 5
- ■ Week 3: 5-3-1
- ■ Week 4: 10-8-6 (and 4-2-2 for the clean and the hex-bar deadlift)

On week 5 you repeat the week 1 workout of 3 × 3 but challenge yourself to do more. Next, you repeat the week 2 workout the same way and so on. You will likely be able to get in three full cycles during a season.

Achieving Progress

Most college strength-training programs try only to maintain strength levels during the season. At the high school level you hope that your competition will adopt that practice. The philosophy of maintaining in college is acceptable because those athletes often have a good base of strength and therefore will not lose much during the season. For example, a college football player benching 400 pounds will be happy with maintaining that level during the season. But the 16-year-old high school junior who is benching 200 pounds is still maturing and can easily gain strength during the season.

Another factor to consider is that a college athlete normally plays only one sport and has a long off-season. But what about that 16-year-old? What if he or she plays several sports? What is the athlete going to do—just maintain all year? Let the competition stagnate. Athletes should go for progress during the season and shouldn't be satisfied with just maintaining.

Finally, consider that not all athletes have to be at peak conditioning during the in-season. Some athletes are red-shirted, and many freshmen will have little opportunity to play. Why not work those athletes harder in the weight room during that time to give them a head start for the next year?

Joe, Deron, and Mike—Strength Training Regimens

Joe's football coach said, "We've got to practice, have meetings, and watch game films. We just don't have time to get in a workout." As a result, Joe lost most of the strength that he had built up over summer. When it came to basketball, Joe's coach said, "Well, we have two games per week plus practices. If football can't lift in-season, we certainly can't." Joe's track coach said, "Weights will screw you up, so we ain't doin' nothin'."

Result? At the end of his freshman year, Joe was at about the same level of strength as he was in his eighth-grade year. This same scenario occurred all four years. At graduation ceremonies, the coaches looked at Joe and said, "He was a good athlete. It's too bad he wasn't bigger, faster, and stronger. Why don't we ever get some mature-looking athletes?" The answer: lack of in-season weight training!

Figure 3.1 Joe's strength level.

Deron's football coach went to hear a major-college strength coach talk about in-season training. "What we want to do is maintain!" said the expert. So that's what the high school coaches did during Deron's football, basketball, and track seasons all four years. Deron spent all his life maintaining. The high school coaches didn't stop to think that the major-college situation was different. At that level athletes play only one sport. Mature college athletes are satisfied with maintaining a 500 squat, 400 bench, and 300 clean over one sport season. But at the high school level, most athletes play two or more sports. High school sophomores may have a 250 squat, 175 bench, and a 160 clean. We don't want to maintain those lifts. To set up a maintenance program in high school is to set up a program of failure. The athletes will never reach their potential.

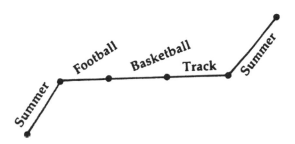

Figure 3.2 Deron's strength level.

Mike's football coach does the BFS in-season program and follows the set-rep system. Gains achieved during the season were not as great as those that occurred in the off-season, but athletes made significant gains throughout each sport season. Because the in-season program was the same for all sports, athletes could make smooth transitions from one sport season to the next. Mike stuck to his program faithfully all four years, broke an average of 400 personal records each year, and reached his potential. His lifts went off the chart!

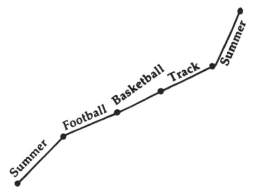

Figure 3.3 Mike's strength level.

One exception to in-season lifting concerns athletes who are in high-stress preseason training, such as football two-a-days. The kids are worn down and mentally and physically exhausted. Adding a lifting program in this situation creates way too much stress.

Mark Eaton, a former center for the Utah Jazz, broke 275 personal records in-season during his rookie year on the BFS program. Mark later became an NBA all-star and two-time Defensive Player of the Year. So get going! It's fun to get stronger. Your athletes will play better, feel better, and be more confident.

Ubly High—Supersizing Athletes

We live in a society in which bigger is often seen as better. Movie theaters have at least a dozen screens, department stores cover entire city blocks, and a combo meal simply isn't enough—you have to have it supersized. This attitude is also prevalent in our school systems, with many parents trying to get their children into bigger schools with vast resources. It's a different story in Ubly, Michigan, where the school has a student body of only 1,000 in grades K-12 and yet offers an exceptional educational and athletic training experience.

© Daniel Delamarter

After implementing the BFS program, the Ubly high school baseball team went on to win the district championships, adopting the slogan "the road to our championship passes through the weight room!"

"Being able to see the kids from as early as the first grade, I have a good understanding as a coach of what they can and cannot do athletically," says Jim Becker, Ubly's Community Schools' head baseball coach and junior varsity football coach. "This perspective is also unique in that we get to see the kids grow up and mature, whereas at bigger schools you often don't know who a kid is until they get into the higher grades."

In 2002 Becker thought he would give the youngest athletes a head start by introducing them to some aspects of the BFS program. "I was thinking, What could these kids do that doesn't take a lot of time or special equipment, but could help their balance, agility and serve as a good warm-up? And it just hit me—Why not the dot drill? From the first day I taught those first graders, right up to where they are now near the end of the school year, I've been amazed at the improvement in their athletic abilities. The dot drill is one of the best warm-up activities I've ever seen."

As for resistance training, Becker says he introduces his athletes to weight training in the seventh grade with the BFS readiness program. "Safety was one of the biggest concerns that the junior high school principal, Michael Smith, had about my program with these kids," says Becker. "I ordered the readiness program, showed it to him, and he was sold right away." The program has proven its worth, Becker explains. "Our safety record is 100 percent—I haven't seen any situations that would require sending a kid to the office."

Becker found that the BFS program was not only safe but also helped the Bearcats prevent injuries. "When I came here I noticed that our football team had quite a number of shoulder injuries on the field. Since we started BFS, for the past two seasons we haven't had a single shoulder injury. So, injury-wise, the BFS program has been a blessing."

When Becker took over the baseball team at Ubly, the outlook for the coming season was pretty bleak—the previous year the team hadn't won a single game and had only one home run the entire season! Says Becker, "I had to take over a team with very low morale—they didn't believe in themselves. The following year, after implementing the BFS program, we had 10 home runs and we doubled the number of doubles, RBIs, and triples. We ended up capturing the district championship." As for football, this year Becker's JV team went 9-0, despite having to play games against several schools with higher classifications. "Now our kids have adopted the slogan 'The road to our championship passes through the weight room.' They believe in the BFS weight program."

With the success of such pro baseball players as Mark McGwire who credit weight training for much of their success, weight training has garnered more acceptance in America's favorite pastime, Becker believes. He says one of the best exercises for baseball is the power clean. "Being a physical education major, I have to ask, 'Why would a baseball player not want to do the power clean? That's the middle part of your body—that's where you work.'"

Much of the recent success of Ubly's athletic programs is also attributable to the support of the school's superintendent, Dave Landeryou. "He's very supportive and helps me get the equipment our athletes need for success," says Becker. "What's funny is that when we first built our weight room I was concerned we had ordered too much equipment in terms of weight. By the end of the year our athletes had become so strong that I had to ask the superintendent to order another 1,000 pounds of weights—and it looks like every year I'm going to need another barbell and more weights."

"Whether it's football, basketball, or baseball, our stands are always packed. And as for education, whenever you get the community involved with the school and the kids believing in themselves, that's when learning is best. That's when good things happen."

CHAPTER

4

BFS Readiness Program

The Bigger Faster Stronger readiness program has been designed for those not yet ready to engage in power weight training performed by more mature athletes. After an athlete goes through the BFS readiness program, he or she will graduate to the BFS regular program of power weight training using free weights. This chapter provides the athlete with a program outlining where to start, how to perform the exercises, how to progress, how to coordinate other athletic activities into a total program, and, finally, how to graduate.

WHO SHOULD USE THE BFS READINESS PROGRAM?

Although many athletes will be ready to jump right into the regular BFS program, several groups of people are more suited to starting with the BFS readiness program.

■ **Junior high school boys and girls.** Most athletes or general physical education students in the seventh grade should begin with the BFS readiness program. We realize that some orthopedic surgeons believe that adolescents of this age are too young to start any kind of weight training. They may say that problems can occur because the bones have not completely hardened. But after careful study, thought, and observation of young athletes who weight train, we believe that the benefits far outweigh any possible risks.

First, without weight training few young people can reach their athletic potential. One of the major—and unfounded—concerns about weight training for young athletes is that it could cause damage to the epiphyseal (growth) plates. Although injury to the epiphyseal plates may cause bone deformity, the risk that this will occur with weight training is no greater than it is with most sports. As for the risk that weight training will stunt growth, premature closing of the epiphyseal plates is related primarily to hormonal influences, not injury. Addressing this subject is Mel Siff, PhD, an exercise scientist whose doctoral thesis examined the biomechanics of soft tissues.

"It has never been shown scientifically or clinically that the periodic imposition of large forces by weight training on the growing body causes damage to the epiphyseal plates," says Siff, in his book *Facts and Fallacies of Fitness*. "It is extremely misleading to focus on the alleged risks of weight training on children when biomechanical research shows that simple daily activities such as running, jumping, striking, or catching can impose far greater forces on the musculoskeletal system than very heavy weight training."

Siff also notes that bone density scans have proven that youngsters who do competitive weightlifting (that is, the snatch and the clean and jerk) have higher bone densities than children who do not use weights, and that clinical research has not shown any correlation between weight training and epiphyseal damage. Siff's comments are supported by an extensive Russian study on young athletes, published in a book titled *School of Height*, which concluded that heavy lifting tends to stimulate bone growth in young athletes rather than inhibit it.

Risk of injury is another area of concern for coaches and parents. Many studies have measured the rate of injuries associated with weight training compared with the rate in other sports. For example, a study published in the November/December 2001 issue of the *Journal of American Academy of Orthopaedic Surgeons* cited research showing that in children ages 5 to 14 years, the number of injuries from bicycling was almost 400 percent greater than the number of injuries from weightlifting. There's more.

In a review paper on resistance training for prepubescent and adolescents published in 2002 in *Strength and Conditioning Coach*, author Mark Shillington reported in a screening of sports-related injuries in school-aged children that resistance training was the likely cause of only 0.7 percent (or 1,576) of injuries compared with 19 percent for football and 15 percent for baseball. Dr. Mel Hayashi, a noted orthopedic surgeon from Thousand Oaks, California, states, "The BFS readiness program should provide great benefits to the junior high athlete. I have no concerns as long as the athlete has good technique." Dr. Hayashi has been a chief orthopedic surgeon at the Olympic Games and is a former chief resident at the Mayo Clinic.

The truth is that weight training and competitive lifting sports are among the safest activities an athlete can participate in. This fact is known worldwide. For example, renowned Russian sports scientist Vladimir Zatsiorsky in his book *Science and Practice of Strength Training* had this to say about the dangers of weight training: "The risk of injury from a well-coached strength training program has been estimated to be about one per 10,000 athlete-exposures," with an athlete-exposure being defined as one athlete taking part in one training session or competition. "Compared to tackle football, alpine skiing, baseball pitching, and even sprint running, strength training is almost free of risk."

The success and popularity of BFS clinics are solid proof of the merits of early weight training. As young athletes strive to achieve the highest levels in competitive sports, they must participate in serious training at a younger age than the champions of the past did. This commitment is the price of success. If young bodies are to handle the stress of this training safely, weight training is essential.

Many strength coaches at major universities throughout the nation have been asked when athletes should start weight training. The vast majority responded, "In junior high." The Eastern Bloc countries start weight training with their athletes at age 12. In addition, we know that weight training is one of the best ways to build self-confidence and self-esteem. A 7th grader can receive just as much satisfaction by going from 85 to 100 pounds on the bench press as a 12th grader can by going from 285 to 300 pounds. Of course, we believe that strict supervision and teaching proper technique is essential to making the BFS readiness program work in junior high school.

■ **High school female athletes.** Some girls go straight into the weight room and lift right with the guys—they are not afraid or intimidated. Even though they use less weight, they match the boys set for set and rep for rep. Our experience, however, tells us that many females of high school age would be better served in large groups by starting their weight training with the BFS readiness program. If a girl cannot do the graduation requirements as outlined in table 4.1, then it is best to start with the BFS readiness program.

■ **High school male athletes.** If an athlete cannot squat to parallel 145 pounds for 10 reps with good form, then we believe it's best for the athlete to start with the BFS readiness program. In September this

The BFS readiness program prepares young athletes for the BFS program by using light weights to teach perfect technique.

program may include as many as 50 percent of 9th graders, 10 to 20 percent of 10th graders, and 5 percent of 11th and 12th graders.

■ **Rehabilitating athletes.** Injured athletes may find the BFS readiness program of great benefit as they rehabilitate. We've found that athletes who have been involved with the BFS program tend to recover faster from injuries than those who did not use the BFS program or those who used other programs. The BFS readiness program uses higher reps and only two sets. Also the strict attention to technique makes this an ideal program for any rehabilitating athlete.

■ **Parents.** Many parents will find the BFS readiness program a great way to get started on a free-weight program, with the added benefit of progressing on the same program that their sons or daughters are using.

BFS READINESS IN JUNIOR HIGH

The BFS readiness program can produce spectacular results in junior high school. The program can be implemented in a physical education class in conjunction with other activities or as a separate entity. Parents and coaches are often surprised to discover how fast seventh graders can learn and profit from this program.

■ **Weight training.** Coaches can teach and stress the technique of the BFS core lifts with just the 45-pound barbell. A two- or three-day-per-week cycle may be used, although I generally recommend two workouts per week, especially in the beginning. Getting three core lifts done in a 40-minute physical education class is easy. On the first day, do box squats, towel benches, and power cleans. On the second workout day, do parallel squats, bench presses, and straight-leg deadlifts. If you have enough time, do auxiliary exercises.

The unique concept of the BFS readiness program is the criteria for increasing poundage. Most programs allow athletes to increase poundage when they do the last set successfully. In our program, they must not only do the prescribed number of sets and reps successfully but also do each set and rep with perfect technique. When the technique of the correct number of sets and reps has been judged perfect, the athlete may increase the weight by five pounds for the workout the following week. This system is amazing for producing great technique early on.

Graduation from the BFS readiness program occurs when a boy can parallel squat 145 pounds for two sets of 10 reps and bench press 105 pounds (or 90 percent of body weight, whichever is less) for two sets of 10 reps (see table 4.1, page 44). If you really get after it, about one out of five students will graduate by the end of the seventh-grade year. After graduation, the athlete would use the standard BFS program. If the emphasis continues throughout the junior high years, many boys will be able to bench press 200, parallel squat 300, and power clean 175 before they enter high school.

■ **Flexibility.** When I coached my son's eighth-grade football team, the whole team did the 9 1/2 minute BFS 1-2-3-4 flexibility program. The parents knew that I expected them to do flexibility exercises every day, and most of the kids did it on their own every day at home. All I had to do was teach it and occasionally check on them. If kids are given a chance to reach their upper limits, it's amazing how many will respond.

■ **Agility.** My son's team also did the BFS dot drill every day on their own. My son did it in 47 seconds, and most of my 31 players did it in less than 60 seconds. Seeing a 13-year-old whip through the BFS dot drill in 50 seconds is impressive.

■ **Speed and plyometrics.** You can teach kids at any age how to run correctly. You want an edge? Teach seventh graders how to run: Less than 1 percent of our nation's seventh graders have had this seemingly basic opportunity.

Teaching kids how to jump is also vital. My son Matt helped me demonstrate plyometrics at a clinic I gave in Georgia. The high school senior basketball players were amazed when Matt jumped from a 20-inch box down to the floor, on to another 20-inch box, then another, and finally hopped up on a 38-inch desk. I was even surprised. Matt said, "Dad, that's nothing." The seniors were reluctant to try until a 13-year-old showed them how.

Questions and Answers

Many elementary schools use the BFS program. Following are some FAQs regarding younger children.

1. When can we start the BFS flexibility program? I taught my third-grade daughter our flexibility program. She mastered it in 15 minutes and began teaching the neighborhood kids. The BFS flexibility program can certainly be taught to all athletes in junior high. If I were a head coach at a high school, I would urge all the local Little League teams to do the flexibility program, even if it went down into the fourth-grade level.

Wouldn't it be advantageous to have every athlete come into high school with great flexibility and with the daily habit of performing a 10-minute flexibility session? Flexibility means injury prevention, and that means speed! In our country, no one does flexibility training properly at early ages. Any coach who can influence the right people to install the BFS flexibility program at the junior high and grade school levels will have an edge, besides providing a great service.

2. When can we start plyometrics? We generally do not teach athletes at any level in this country how to jump. All we do when we test an athlete on a vertical jump is say, "Jump as high as you can!" Athletes must master definite techniques to reach their maximum. We can and should teach grade school and junior high athletes the techniques of the vertical jump and the standing long jump. As for plyometric drills, I see no reason why we cannot incorporate basic plyometric drills in the total junior high conditioning program. Two 10-minute sessions per week on plyometrics can pay big dividends by the time those athletes go into the high school program.

3. When can we start teaching the BFS sprint technique system? I don't believe you can start too soon. The longer an athlete is allowed to run incorrectly, the harder it will be for him or her to unlearn bad habits and learn correct technique. As I worked with NBA hopefuls at tryout camp for the Utah Jazz and with players for the Sacramento Kings, I asked them about their previous work with flexibility, plyometrics, and sprint training. It was zilch. Zero! NBA players usually have poor flexibility (LaSalle Thompson of the Kings was an exception). I asked them if they wanted greater flexibility and if they would have liked to learn how to run at an early age. Of course, they all said yes.

4. How is the readiness program different from the high school program? There is little difference. The seventh grader can do the same flexibility program, the same agility drills, the same beginning plyometrics, and the same sprint-technique system. The only real difference is in the lifting program, although both programs use the same core lifts and the same concept in selecting auxiliary exercises.

5. What results can we expect from the readiness program? When coaches who seek excellence choose the BFS readiness program, their athletes will accomplish great things. I promise that a high school with an enrollment of 1,000 can expect 25 athletes to come from the junior high each year with these abilities: a minimum 300-pound parallel squat with great form, a minimum 200-pound bench, and a minimum 175-pound clean with great form. These players will also possess great flexibility, good plyometric ability, and correct running form. With these abilities come great side benefits, such as increased self-confidence, good work habits, and a winning attitude. One thing that amazes me is the great number of schools who will do nothing again this year. We have the technology available. Let's use it. Get the edge!

BFS READINESS—WEIGHT TRAINING

To minimize the risk of injury from any conditioning program, coaches must teach proper technique. During BFS clinics our clinicians not only teach athletes how to lift and spot properly but also instruct coaches how to teach the proper lifting and spotting techniques. As the proverb goes, "Give a man a fish and you feed him for a day. Teach a man to fish and you feed him for a lifetime." With that in mind, here are the details of the BFS readiness weight-training program.

Beginning

Start with just the 45-pound Olympic bar on each core lift. Do not worry if this amount of weight is light and does not seem challenging. We are going to test for two things: First, can you perform two sets of 5 or 10 reps, and second, can you perform each rep and each set with great technique? We want you to work on perfect technique, especially at first. Therefore, if 45 pounds is too heavy (which might be the case on the hang clean or the bench press) start with less. Don't feel bad if you have to start with less—it doesn't matter where you *start*, only where you *finish*!

Progressing

Two things must happen before you progress to greater weight. You must be able to complete your two sets of 10 or 5 reps and be able to do each rep of each set with perfect technique. When you can do these two things, you may go up five pounds the next week on the same lift.

Now record the date of your successful workout (see figure 4.1). All serious weight-trained athletes keep records. You should do the same. You will have pride and satisfaction as you work up in poundage toward graduation. If you cannot do the two sets of 10 or 5 reps with perfect technique, you must keep repeating the same weight until you can.

Judging Technique

A coach, parent, or training partner should judge an athlete's technique. When athletes train alone, obviously they will have to judge themselves. I encourage everyone to train with a partner, for three reasons: The partner can motivate the lifter, spot the lifter, and judge the lifter's technique.

There are three judging rules for each lift. If the lifter breaks any one of the rules during any set, he or she may not progress next week.

Bench and Towel Bench Press

Athletes should perform two sets of 10 reps each.

■ **Touch the chest.** If the bar doesn't touch the chest or towel, it doesn't count.

■ **Even extension.** We do not want one arm going up way before the other arm, but a little disparity is acceptable. Also, look for uneven elbows at the bottom position. Sometimes one elbow is tucked into the chest while the other is out to the side. Don't count it! Force the athlete to do it right.

■ **Hips down.** By using a wide stance, with the feet underneath and shoulders forced toward the hips, the athlete will be less likely to arch (lift the hips up from bench). We believe that all lifters, especially young lifters, should observe this rule because it will give them better chest development.

BIGGER FASTER STRONGER BFS

READINESS RECORD CARD

Name:________________________

Height:_______Weight:_______Age:_______

Pds.	Box Squat	Towel Bench	Power Clean	Hex-Bar Deadlift	Parallel Squat	Bench Press
15						
20						
25						
30						
35						
40						
45						
50						
55						
60						
65						
70						
75						
80						
85						
90						
95			Girl's Graduation			Girl's Graduation
100						

Figure 4.1 BFS readiness record card.

Box Squat

Athletes should perform two sets of 10 reps each.

■ **Arched lower back.** The lower back must be locked in, not rounded.

■ **Pause on the box.** The athlete must sit on the box and rock back slightly before driving forward and up. If the athlete just touches the box and comes up, the lift doesn't count.

■ **Finish the lift.** At the finish of the lift, the athlete must come up on the toes as he or she would during a jump.

Squat

Athletes should perform two sets of 10 reps each.

■ **Arched lower back.** The lower back must be locked in, not rounded.

■ **Depth.** The athlete must squat down until the tops of the thighs are at least parallel with the floor. Many beginning lifters will find this very difficult.

■ **Stance, knees, and toes.** The stance should look like an athlete's stance, not narrow or wide. Watch the toes—a 45-degree angle is too much. Also, watch the knees. If they come too far in on the way up, do not count the lift.

Power Clean

Athletes should perform two sets of five reps each.

■ **Arched back.** In the starting position, the lower back should be locked in.

■ **Acceleration.** The athlete should pull the bar off the floor slowly, then jump with the bar close to the body. Elbows should be high, with the chin away from the chest.

■ **Catch position.** The lifter must rack the bar to deltoids properly and be in an athletic position.

Straight-Leg Deadlift

Athletes should perform two sets of 10 reps each.

■ **Speed.** The athlete should perform the lift slowly and with control.

■ **Weight selection.** Maximum poundage should be 55 pounds.

Organization

The BFS readiness program takes only 45 minutes two times per week. A maximum of five athletes should use one barbell, allowing one to lift, three to spot, and one to get ready. The athletes should rotate in order.

If the program is part of a physical education class, the class could be divided into three groups, with the groups rotating every 15 minutes.

For example, group 1 does core lifts, group 2 does auxiliary lifts, and group 3 does agility and running skills.

The equipment needed to conduct this program for 15 athletes is as follows:

Approximate cost:	
Olympic bench press	$199
Squat rack	349
Squat box	49
Three economy 300-pound sets	477
BFS training plates	59
	$1,133

The cost goes up about $150 for each additional group of five athletes. The equipment suggestions are for heavy-duty equipment meant for years of constant use. Equipment for home use would be less expensive.

Graduation

Graduation depends on performance, not age, which is as it should be. Some children mature faster than others do, and some learn technique faster. Graduation requirements favor the bigger and heavier athlete to some extent. You will see in table 4.1 that a male athlete must do two sets of 10 reps with 145 pounds on the squat, and a female must do 105 pounds. Everyone starts with 45 pounds and goes up at a maximum rate of 5 pounds a week.

Graduation requirements are based on three lifts: the squat, bench, and hang clean. An athlete must pass all three lifts to graduate (see table 4.1). Although they are important lifts, the box squat, towel bench, and straight-leg deadlifts are not included in graduation requirements. Graduation means that the athlete is ready to begin the regular BFS program, a more strenuous program requiring a more mature frame. The total BFS program allows all athletes to reach their potential soon enough.

Awards

Giving awards for graduation from the BFS readiness program will make graduation special and develop pride of accomplishment. Awards might be ribbons, medals, shirts, or simply placing the athletes' names on a chart. Give an award for each event passed.

Table 4.1 Graduation Requirements

Event	Male	Female
Squat (2 sets of 10 reps)	145 lb	75 lb
Bench (2 sets of 10 reps)	105 lb or 90% of body weight	75 lb or 90% of body weight
Power clean (2 sets of 5 reps)	105 lb or 90% of body weight	75 lb or 90% of body weight

PART II

Strength Exercises

Six Absolutes of Perfect Technique

BFS has developed six training principles, or absolutes, that are amazingly effective in teaching perfect technique, not only in the weight room but also in any sport. Coaches who learn the six BFS absolutes can dramatically elevate their athletes' strength and their own coaching ability. These are the six absolutes.

1. **Use an athletic or jump stance.**
2. **Be tall.**
3. **Spread the chest (lock in the lower back).**
4. **Align the toes.**
5. **Align the knees (knees over toes).**
6. **Keep your eyes on target.**

One reason the six absolutes are so effective is that they encourage participating coaches to use the same terminology when teaching weight training and sport skills. After all, how can coaches expect athletes to follow instructions exactly when the information they receive varies from coach to coach? Such confusion also goes against the concept of developing a unified program. Therefore, instead of one coach saying, "Make your chest big!" when teaching the squat and another coach saying, "Spread the chest!" at batting practice, both coaches should agree to say, "Spread the chest."

USING THE ATHLETIC OR JUMP STANCE

When talking about stances, many coaches talk about moving the feet "about shoulder-width apart" or "narrower than hip-width." That phrasing will no longer be acceptable, because coaches will make sure that everything in the program is relevant to athletics.

When I coach athletes, I explain that all sports require the same two basic stances—the jump stance and the athletic stance. Whether it's tennis, softball, or football, the stances are the same. Athletes use the jump stance primarily when lifting from the floor with such lifts as the power clean, snatch, and hex-bar deadlift. They use an athletic stance in lifts like the squat or in the rack position in the power clean (when they catch the bar on the shoulders).

At clinics I ask the athletes to pretend that I'm their little brother. I say I am a shortstop or linebacker. I get into various stances—narrow, wide, toes out, and just right. From that perspective, every athlete and coach can immediately differentiate between a goofy stance and a good stance (the athletic stance). Next, I ask the athletes and coaches to look at my feet as I step up to a line to do a standing long jump. Again, I get into various stances. They can easily identify the jump stance from among my examples. The upshot is that athletes want to look like someone who is either ready to hit or ready to jump. Athletes must be in an athletic position or a jump position, in the athletic stance or the jump stance.

Let's take a closer look at how this absolute works in squatting. In squatting, lifters use three basic squatting stances—bodybuilding, power-lifting, and athletic.

■ **Bodybuilding stance.** Bodybuilders generally use a very narrow stance, often with the toes straight ahead and sometimes with a board placed underneath the heels. They use this method to attain certain bodybuilding objectives of increasing development of the teardrop-shaped muscle of the lower thigh called the vastus medialis.

■ **Power-lifting stance.** Many power lifters use a very wide stance with the toes flared out, a stance I refer to as a power-lifting stance. But some power lifters use a narrow stance, with the toes pointed outward quite a lot. And a few power lifters use an athletic stance. Power lifters choose whatever stance allows them to squat the most weight, although some of those techniques significantly increase the risk of knee and hip injuries.

Whenever I read about squatting stances from strength coaches or attend a seminar on the subject, the experts invariably say, "Take about a shoulder-width stance." This comment is meant to refer to an athletic stance, but is there a better way to communicate? Yes! This is part of your winning edge, part of the "secret."

Coaches routinely ask basketball players to get in a "rebounding stance," baseball players to "look like a shortstop," football players to get in a "linebacker stance," and volleyball and tennis players to assume their "ready position." At BFS clinics we get into a bodybuilder's squatting stance and ask, "Does this look like a linebacker?" The kids say, "No. Get your feet wider!" We then get into a wide power-lifting stance with the toes flared way out and ask, "How about this position? Does this look like a football, basketball, or baseball player?" Everyone laughs. Then we get into an athletic stance, and everyone realizes that the "ready position" for all mainstream high school sports is essentially the same.

■ **Athletic stance.** As athletes spot each other, they should make sure that their teammates always look like authentic athletes with their stances. Athletes build their power and strength from the athletic stance. Calling for the athletic stance is a far superior terminology than saying "about shoulder-width." Our way also sends a message that all participants are athletes and ensures that their squatting stance remains the same when they make a transition from basketball to baseball or from volleyball to softball (see figures 5.1a and b). The jump stance, similar to the athletic stance, prepares an athlete to be explosive when he jumps.

Figure 5.1 *(a)* Athletic stance *(b)* Jump stance.

BEING TALL

You need to be tall all the time, whether you're sitting, walking, sprinting, lifting, or even stretching. You can't slump or lean forward outside your center of gravity and expect to perform well. Being tall produces dramatic improvements in posture, improvements that will translate into better sport performance and reduced risk of injury.

Here's a simple test to determine if you're standing tall. Stand with your heels, buttocks, back, shoulders, and head against a wall. Now try to slide one hand behind your lower back, at bellybutton level or at the great arch in your back (approximately bellybutton level). If you are standing tall, the thickest part of your hand will just fill the gap between the wall and your back. If your hand either slides right through or becomes stuck, you are probably not standing tall.

As a coach, you can determine if your athletes are standing tall simply by observing their relaxed standing posture. Look at each of them from the side and note the position of the shoulder and head. Does the head thrust forward? Are the knees locked? Is the pelvis thrust forward? If the answer to any of these questions is yes, the athlete is not being tall.

Athletes who stand tall look like winners. When an athlete is tall, the waist will appear flatter and the shoulders broader. In fact, the common reaction from friends to athletes who learn to be tall is that they've lost weight! In sports that include an aesthetic component, such as diving or figure skating, the postural improvements from being tall will produce higher scores from the judges. Further, the postural improvements from being tall can help prevent the lower-back problems that have become an epidemic among our population.

If an athlete is slouching, say, "Be tall." Immediately, good things happen. If an athlete is bending at the waist with a rounded back, the quickest way to correct this problem is to say, "Be tall." Fine-tuning comes with the other absolutes, especially keeping eyes on target and spreading the chest. All these terms are designed to help athletes get into a correct and efficient alignment.

Athletes should apply the be-tall absolute with most lifts in the weight room. In squatting, they need to squat with the feeling of sitting tall. They do not want to bend over with the head down and hips high, because doing so can injure the lower back and will not develop functional strength (see figures 5.2 and 5.3).

Athletes must also be tall outside the weight room. In track and field, sprinters must sprint tall to maximize their speed. In throwing a discus or ball, athletes must be tall. Leaning or bending forward causes technique problems and inefficiency.

Figure 5.2   Poor squatting position.

Figure 5.3   Good squatting position. Note how the athlete is lifting tall.

At BFS clinics athletes thoroughly learn the absolute of being tall by the end of the day. Coaches in attendance who coach their own kids use the six absolutes repeatedly. We always find it rewarding to see the rapid improvements in both coaches and athletes, especially in coaches who have no significant background in weight training. In just one day they become amazingly skilled in correcting technique flaws. Coaches should make sure that their athletes are being tall in all they do.

SPREADING THE CHEST

I discovered this fantastic coaching secret while doing a BFS clinic. I was frustrated because several boys could not lock in their lower backs. I blurted out, "Spread the chest!" To my amazement, the position of these boys' lower backs immediately went from poor to great. I now say, "Spread the chest" to athletes when they dead lift or power clean. Once athletes experience locking the lower back into place as they spread the chest while sitting in a chair, they can usually have the same experience without the chair. Sitting in the chair just makes it easier. Several years later I noticed that some strength coaches were saying, "Get a big chest." It is the same principle, but "spread the chest" has proved to be a superior coaching term.

Spreading the chest and locking in the lower back go hand in hand, but you must visualize and coach both. The lower back must swoop way in, into a deeply concave position. Most coaches have a difficult time seeing the difference between fair, good, and great concave lower-back position. When athletes spread their chests, the lower back will start to lock in properly in a concave position.

Matt Shepard is shown in figure 5.4 trying to hit a home run. Think he can do it? How about in figure 5.5? Does he have a better chance in that position? It's a no-brainer, right? OK, then how do you fix the problem and help all athletes go from wherever they are now to a rating of 10? Simple! Use the six absolutes.

Two coaching guidelines can help athletes who have difficulty getting the kinesthetic feel for the correct position. First, have them put their hands on their knees with some pressure, as in figure 5.6 (page 54). Most of the small percentage who were unable to get the kinesthetic feel will be successful from this position. Have those who still cannot get into correct position sit on a bench or squat box as in figure 5.7 (page 54). Now, again say, "Be tall and spread the chest." You might have to mold them by pushing in on the lower back and pulling back on the shoulders, but they should be able to do it.

Figure 5.4 Example of poor stance; note the rounded back.

Figure 5.5 Proper batting stance.

From this sitting position, which should look good by now, the athletes squat up a few inches and see if they can stay in the correct position. Some will be able to do it and some won't. Those who still have a problem simply start over. The last step is to have them stand erect. Tell them to try to remember the correct position and then do it. Again, those who still can't attain the correct position should start over on the box. Most of the time, even if I have 100 athletes, none of them needs to start over.

The athletes and coaches will hear the words "spread the chest" several hundred times at a BFS clinic. Afterward, athletes will need to be corrected throughout the entire school year. The phrase should just be part of everyone's vocabulary. Also, in the weight room every spotter has the duty of making sure that whoever is lifting is using perfect technique. If the lower back is even 1 percent away from perfect, coaches and athletes should issue the command "Be tall and spread the chest." In any activity you coach, you will have better athletes who will be far less injury prone if the lower back is correct. All you have to say is "Spread the chest."

Figure 5.6 Getting the kinetic feel for proper alignment.

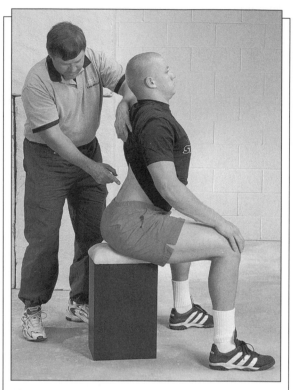

Figure 5.7 Good alignment is important, even when sitting.

ALIGNING THE TOES

Although it may sound strange, you should strive to align the toes of your athletes. What this means is that the toes should be either straight ahead (jump stance) or pointed slightly out for balance (athletic stance). I call this absolute "toes aligned." Whether an athlete is lifting, sprinting, jumping, or stretching, the toes must be aligned.

Coaches and athletes constantly neglect correct toe alignment in stretching. Athletes must get the toes right in everything they do, every time they do it, so that correct toe alignment becomes a habit. For example, the athlete in figure 5.8 is demonstrating one of the BFS stretches on the wall (back-leg stretch). Note that the toes of the back foot are pointed out. This common error can be easily corrected. Figure 5.9 shows this stretch being done correctly. Notice the difference.

Figures 5.10 and 5.11 (page 56) demonstrate toe alignment of the front foot in our BFS hip-flexor stretch. The toes should not point out, as shown in figure 5.10, but should be straight, as shown in figure 5.11. Coaches can correct improper alignment by shouting, "Toes!" Teammates of this athlete should also shout, "Toes!"

This technique "secret" is fairly well known, but it's still the explanation behind many mistakes that athletes make. Most athletes point their toes out naturally because doing so aids in balance. But athletes often point their toes out too far. No problem. All you do is go back to the athletic stance formula. Ask the question, "Do you look like a linebacker, shortstop, or basketball player?" Remember, maximum power comes from an exact athletic stance, which, of course, includes pointing the toes out only slightly.

By using the toes-aligned absolute, coaches will quickly see huge improvements in overall technique. Insist that all athletes act as assistant coaches and coach their teammates when spotting or performing any phase of strength and conditioning. If your goal is to win, then all athletes and coaches must be unified in helping each other become great. When I

© Claus Andersen

Superior sprinting mechanics, including proper knee alignment, is one reason Tim Montgomery broke the world record of 100 meters in 9.78 seconds.

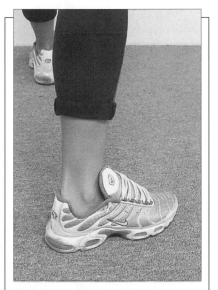

Figure 5.8 Toes improperly aligned in the back-leg stretch.

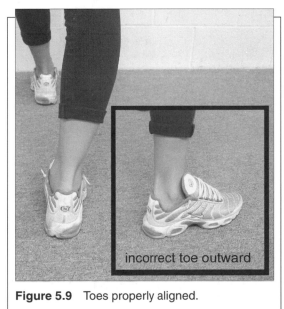

incorrect toe outward

Figure 5.9 Toes properly aligned.

Figure 5.10 Hip flexor stretch with toes to the side in an improper alignment.

Figure 5.11 Hip flexor stretch with toes aligned correctly.

see athletes lift or perform other phases of strength training and conditioning, ensuring correct toe alignment is a constant challenge. But with proper and frequent application of the toes-aligned absolute, meeting this challenge becomes much easier.

ALIGNING THE KNEES

The knees must always be over the toes in the weight room, in every phase of strength training and conditioning, in every drill, and in every athletic movement. The most common problem is that athletes let their knees come together, putting pressure on the medial collateral ligament. This fault is especially prevalent among female athletes and junior high boys.

Athletes may use many incorrect positions for the knees during lifts and stretches. Be alert and correct these faults immediately

Many times the knees will be far in front of the toes. Athletes must learn to balance on the entire foot. The heels should not come up because doing so puts too much pressure on the patella area, besides being ineffective. To help correct this problem, use the partner system and have the athletes practice squatting with the hips back and the knees as straight as possible vertically. Alternatively, have them try a front squat with very light weight. This method will help athletes practice the art of stabilizing the body correctly.

In going through the training (use athletic stance, be tall, spread the chest, align the knees and toes, and keep eyes on target), athletes learn to sit with the hips well back. This position keeps the knees aligned over the toes.

Knees out or knees in is also a problem. Squatting with knees out will put unwanted pressure on the lateral collateral ligaments. The knees-out problem is easy to correct: Simply widen the athlete's stance until the knees are aligned directly over the toes. More common among female athletes, the knees-in problem (see figure 5.12) puts unwanted pressure on the medial collateral ligaments. The knees-in problem is more difficult to correct than the knees-out fault. The first step is to yell, "Knees!" to athletes while they are squatting or doing some other lift to signal them to force the knees out over the toes. This signal may or may not work the first time. If it doesn't, the second correction technique is to tap lightly on the inside of the athlete's knee. This kinesthetic approach gives the athlete a feel for the problem. The cure usually happens after only a few light taps. If the problem persists, videotaping the athletes will allow them to see the problem. This combination of coaching guidelines will usually do the trick.

Figure 5.12 Knees-in position—incorrect technique, the knees should be over the toes.

Figure 5.13   Knees aligned—correct technique.

Knees that are in perfect alignment (scoring a 10) will be straight from every position. In my clinics I place the top end of a ruler at the middle of the athlete's knee. The bottom of the ruler should be at the middle of the athlete's toes. If the ruler is inside or outside, the position is incorrect. Sometimes the knees will be outside the toes, usually because of a narrow stance. Simply widen the athlete's stance to cure this problem. Figure 5.13 shows the proper knees-aligned position.

Remember that you can use this absolute when coaching any activity—running, jumping, stretching, or in sports practice. If they keep their knees over their toes, your athletes will perform better and experience fewer injuries (especially to the knees). Positive things will happen when your athletes learn this vital coaching absolute—align the knees.

KEEPING THE EYES ON TARGET

The eyes-on-target absolute is especially useful in sports like football. For example, suppose you are behind late in the game. You're on defense and must create a turnover. Instead of tackling after having kept your eyes on the ball carrier's chest, you could try switching to targeting the ball. At BFS clinics athletes learn this absolute so thoroughly that by the end of the day you can simply say "Eyes," and an immediate perfect correction takes place. Figures 5.14 and 5.15 illustrate examples of the eyes-on-target absolute.

Eyes on target is a great tool to use in the weight room, especially in our example of squats. When an athlete looks up at the ceiling while beginning the squatting movement at the top position, everything might seem comfortable and right. The bottom position is where things go wrong. Looking at the same point on the ceiling when in the bottom position is virtually impossible. Therefore, the eyes move, the head moves, and the body moves out of position. The lifter must not look down at the ground because doing so can be as dangerous as tackling a ball carrier with the head down (in figure skating, a commonly used expression is "Look at the ice, fall on the ice!"). Most lifts require the eyes to be focused straight ahead but there are exceptions. During cleans and the hex-bar deadlift the eyes should be slightly above horizontal: During the sprint start, they are at 45 degrees. See figure 5.16.

Eyes on target is one of the coaching secrets that will give you a big edge on your opponents. Use it often.

Study these teaching points, write them down, post them in your weight room, and memorize them. Use the six BFS absolutes consistently in all your programs and you'll see a remarkable difference.

Figure 5.14 Perfect stretch position with eyes on target.

Figure 5.15 In the hex-bar deadlift the eyes should look slightly above the horizontal line.

Figure 5.16 Proper head position in sprint start.

Squat and Squat Variations

The parallel squat is the king of all exercises. If athletes do nothing but parallel squats, they will have a good program—not great, but good. Conversely, if they leave out the squats, minimize them, or perform them incorrectly, it won't matter what type of exercises they perform, what machines they use, or what training system they follow. Without the squat, athletes cannot fulfill their athletic potential.

The parallel squat builds the foundation for great speed, regardless of the size of the athlete. A six-foot-four, 265-pound football player who has good athletic ability can run a 40-yard dash in 4.6 seconds if he practices the squat. If that athlete does some other type of free-weight exercise or substitutes a machine for the squat, he will be lucky to run a 40 in 5.0 seconds.

The value of squats in creating an athletic edge is even greater for females, because many female athletes today still do little serious weight training or none at all. (Some females may avoid doing the squat because they mistakenly believe that it will make their thighs too big. They have yet to learn that female bodies build muscle to a lesser degree than male bodies do.) After you read this chapter, you'll see why parallel squats are critical for all athletes.

Although most high school weight-training programs include squats, many allow their athletes to squat way too high. In an eight-team conference, probably four to five schools will squat high. Even the two or three schools that have their athletes squat low enough will often have serious technique or spotting problems that decrease the effectiveness of the exercise and increase the risk of injury. You can make a quantum leap over your opponents by performing the parallel squat correctly.

KNEES AND SQUATS

Are squats bad for the knees? Despite evidence to the contrary, people raise this question constantly, even people who have no connection to athletics or physical education. What is behind the controversy? In the past several decades many football coaches and orthopedic surgeons have taken a firm stand that squats and football do not go together. At the other extreme, track and field athletes, especially shot-putters and hammer, javelin, and discus throwers, have been doing heavy squats for years with no apparent knee damage. Olympic lifters and power lifters seldom experience knee problems. Furthermore, some Asian and Eastern cultures require sitting in a deep squat position for hours, and no apparent knee problems result.

I have always found it odd that these two extreme views exist. Formal research studies that might clear up the controversy have not been undertaken. In the absence of firm data, the antisquat camp has had to base its stand generally on hearsay or opinion.

The prosquat camp seems to base its stand generally on personal experience. I formed my position because I performed competition squats for nearly 15 years without knee problems and because I have observed thousands of athletes. In the summer of 1971 I conducted an intense project to uncover the facts about squats. I researched numerous research journals, physical education journals, and medical journals dating back to 1950. Incredible as it may seem, I could locate practically no pertinent scientific research regarding squats and knees, or even exercise and knees.

The lack of published research was frustrating. From my several decades of experience I know that performing squats by descending under complete control to achieve a parallel position results in many positive changes, such as the following:

- The lower-body muscles become stronger and bigger, especially the quadriceps and hamstrings.
- The tendons become thicker and stronger.
- The knee ligaments become thicker and stronger.
- The entire articular capsule of the knee becomes thicker.

■ The bones of the legs become stronger and slightly bigger because of increased capillarization.

■ The cartilage of the knee becomes more resistant to injury.

These positive effects explain why athletes who do squats correctly have far fewer knee injuries than those who do not squat at all. Including squats and performing them properly is especially important for female athletes, because they are up to five times more likely to suffer knee injuries than men are in sports such as basketball and volleyball. According to the American Orthopedic Society for Sports Medicine, each year approximately 20,000 high school girls suffer serious knee injuries, most involving the anterior cruciate ligament, which helps stabilize the knee (see figure 6.1).

Proper squatting technique offers athletes the best defense against knee injuries. That being said, deep squats can present some danger to the knee joint, especially if the lifter comes down fast, is out of control, or bounces at the bottom position. Common sense tells us that a football player who does deep squats with, say, 400 pounds is asking for problems if he comes down hard and bounces at the deep bottom position. But if an athlete lifting the

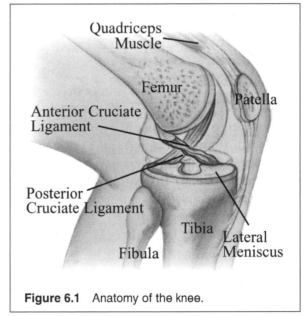

Figure 6.1 Anatomy of the knee.

same weight comes down under control to the parallel-squat position and then comes up, the knee joint should be in no danger whatsoever. This is a completely natural movement, like sitting in a chair. Bones, ligaments, and muscles in the human body were designed and constructed to be able to articulate to a parallel-squat position.

The evidence shows that performing squats correctly greatly reduces the number of knee injuries in athletes. Our files are full of coaches' feedback that relates how dramatically the number of injuries decreased after they included squats in their training programs. Believe me, if there were a problem with squats, we'd hear about it. We are resolute in our belief that performing squats correctly is like taking out an insurance policy against injury, especially knee injury.

SQUAT DEPTH

Understanding the importance of depth in squats is imperative. We base our standards on a parallel depth or slightly below it. The high school all-American standard is 500 pounds for males with heavy builds and 325 pounds for females with heavy builds. The all-state standard is 400 pounds for males and 235 pounds (think two plates and a collar) for females. BFS set those standards to help athletes and coaches understand when an athlete achieves something unique. Only a special athlete with special understanding of how to do squats can reach those standards. If an athlete squats a foot high or three inches high with 500 pounds, it is meaningless. Not a whole lot is really happening, and the athlete will miss out on great benefits.

Coaches and athletes must also understand that improvement in running speed relates directly to hamstring development, which correct squatting technique will accomplish superbly. Squatting high will strengthen only the quadriceps, the muscles in the front part of the upper leg. Not until the thighs are parallel or slightly below parallel will the hamstrings be positively affected. As the athlete attains proper depth, the hamstrings and the quadriceps will be strengthened in a coordinated, functional manner. To improve speed, the hamstrings must become stronger. Squatting to the proper depth will give athletes a big edge over their opponents.

PRESQUAT TECHNIQUE

Before squatting, you must make several important technique preparations—getting a secure grip, properly positioning the bar on the shoulders, and removing the barbell from the rack.

■ **Grip.** Two technique guidelines will help you establish a proper grip on the squat. First is thumb position. Should you have your thumb around the bar or behind the bar? About 60 percent of power lifters have the thumb in back, and 40 percent prefer their thumbs around the bar. Obviously, both styles are acceptable, but I prefer that my athletes lift with their thumbs behind the bar. I feel that this style is superior because it tends to prevent the bar from slipping off the shoulders and down the back. The bar seems to be more secure with the thumbs in back, but if after trying both styles an athlete prefers to have the thumbs around the bar, I don't object.

The second grip guideline to consider is the width of the grip. This is another of those secrets that can give you an edge. At clinics I ask those attending to pretend that they have a bar on their shoulders and to get a "very narrow grip." Then, I ask them to sit tall, spread their chests, and lock in their lower backs. Next, I tell them to change to a wide grip and lock in their lower backs. Then I ask, "Which grip makes it easier to lock in the lower back?" Unanimously, they say that it's the wide grip.

Make sure to use the lines grooved into most Olympic bars about four inches from the inside collars. Use these lines as reference points. For example, you might put your first finger on each line with your thumbs behind the bar. Now you are properly balanced with a wide grip and have some assurance that the bar will remain secure on your shoulders. You are now ready to place the bar on your shoulders. Figure 6.2 illustrates the proper way to grip.

■ **Bar position.** A common mistake for athletes who squat is placing the bar too high on the shoulders. In fact, many athletes place the bar right on the neck. That hurts, so they'll use a barbell pad. Most athletes can squat with more weight, greater effectiveness, and more comfort by placing the bar lower on the shoulders. Structural differences in bone length and tendon-muscle attachments may allow some athletes to squat more effectively with high bar placement.

Some power lifters place the bar extremely low on the shoulders, perhaps as much as four inches from the top of the shoulders. This method may give a slight anatomical advantage, or the advantage may result from using a heavy, tight lifting suit or even from a lack of flexibility. Whatever the reason, squatting using extremely low bar placement detracts from overall leg development, which is obviously not helpful to the athlete.

Figure 6.2 Perfect bar placement for the squat.

Most athletes will be able to find a natural groove on the shoulders when they come under the bar in a proper position. We tell them, "Don't put the bar on your neck; put it on your shoulders. Find a groove." In almost every case, if a coach voices these technique cues, athletes will achieve excellent bar placement during their squats.

■ **Removing the bar from the rack.** I've seen high school athletes get all psyched up to squat and then position their shoulders two to three inches under the bar. Next, with an explosive movement, they jam their shoulders against the bar. Well, jamming their shoulders against a steel bar from that distance causes bruises on the necks or shoulders. Besides feeling pain, these athletes often place the bar on their shoulders incorrectly. I've also seen athletes whip a bar off the rack. Many times these athletes are not in solid squatting position as they back up to a ready stance. For those reasons, the few injuries that take place during squatting most often occur while the athlete is taking the bar off the rack or replacing it on the rack, not during the squat exercise itself.

A far superior way to handle the bar is to come under it in a solid power position, making sure that everything is correct (refer to figure 6.2). To accomplish this, get the bar in the groove on your shoulders. Look straight ahead and spread the chest. The next technique point is critical. Get into your athletic stance directly under the bar. Many athletes stand a foot back and lean forward. Taking that position can cause lower-back trouble, especially with heavy weight. Now you're ready. Put some pressure on the bar and make sure that everything feels right. If it does, blast off! This explosive movement will not bruise your shoulders because you've already put some pressure on the bar. Because of your explosive movement from the correct position, the bar feels light. You are confident.

The bar is now off the rack, and you are firmly under the weight. At this point, take a short step back with each foot and resume an athletic stance. You are ready to squat. With some squat racks, you may have to take several steps backward to clear yourself to squat. Some step-squat racks and peg-squat racks may require many long steps for clearance. Some squat racks have a spotting tier that is too high for parallel squats, thus requiring a long walk back to reach the correct position. Obviously, you are at a disadvantage if you have to do anything more than take a short step back with each foot.

SQUAT TECHNIQUE

Before teaching proper squatting technique, I want to explain the difference between controlled psych and frenzied psych. I've seen some power lifters work themselves into a screaming psychotic frenzy when attempting an all-time max. They invariably miss and sometimes get hurt. The parallel squat can be a tricky lift. Technique and correct position mean everything. You must execute every technique guideline to perfection when attempting a new max. You must be psyched, but it must be a controlled psych. You must be thinking about correct positioning throughout the entire lift. Now, on to the squat.

The squat has four main phases: the start, the descent, the bottom position, and the upward drive. You must concentrate on perfect technique during all parts of the squat to achieve maximum results.

1. Start. You should be looking straight ahead at a target. Your mind should be clear and intense, thinking about technique: spreading the chest, locking in the lower back, and performing your descent pattern. You must take a huge breath and hold it just before the descent. For a one-rep max, I recommend taking two breaths—first, a huge breath you hold to let the air settle deep within the rib cavity, and second, a quick breath as you begin the descent to expand the chest even further (figure 6.3a).

2. Descent. You should descend in an even, controlled pattern. Some athletes descend inch by inch and take forever, which is a mistake. Some athletes rapidly crash down out of control, which is dangerous. By using an even, controlled pattern, your technique will likely be better.

Throughout the descent, you should hold your breath. You, your coach, and your spotters should be mindful of all previously discussed technique guidelines. Always spread the chest, lock in the lower back, look at your target, and sit tall (figure 6.3b).

3. Bottom position. You should squat to the parallel position or slightly below it. Keep in mind that many athletes squat high, a common flaw that will detract from their performance. By adhering strictly to the parallel position, you will have an advantage in competition. If you squat high, only minimal hamstring or glute development will take place, which will limit your improvement in speed and jumping. Hitting a correct parallel position is critical for personal and team success. It is one of the great secrets in this book.

Most athletes find it difficult to know when they are parallel. Spotters need to become involved in letting their partners know when they are parallel. The marble test is effective here.

I use the marble test because it helps athletes visualize a true parallel-squat position. I squat down to a position four inches from parallel and ask, "Now pretend that I have a marble on the top of my thigh halfway between my knee and hip. What would it do?" Naturally, they say it would roll down toward my knee. My position illustrates a squat that is too high. When I squat parallel, the athletes can visualize the marble staying in the middle of my thigh.

Spotters, who act also as judges, should position themselves to see their partner's thighs while they're squatting. The spotters should let their partners know exactly how they are doing on every rep as they visualize that marble. Saying things like "You're one inch too high," "You're at perfect depth," or "You're too low" can be very helpful.

Power lifters must break parallel. Therefore, the marble would have to roll toward the athlete's hip. Some football and strength coaches want their athletes to break parallel. I have no objection to this whatsoever. The bottom line is that to get proper leg development, athletes must go at least to parallel (figure 6.3c).

Some coaches use the bottom of the thigh, not the top of the thigh, as their parallel-squatting reference point. This method creates problems because many athletes with large thighs end up squatting two or three inches higher than they would if they used the top of the thigh as the parallel point. These athletes will forgo hamstring and glute development; in addition, standards become meaningless.

4. Upward drive. You should continue holding your breath when beginning the upward drive from the parallel position. You should picture your hips attached to a giant rubber band. As you go down to parallel, you stretch the rubber band to the limit. The instant your hips hit parallel, you release the rubber band. Your hips pop upward while you maintain perfect technique.

Figure 6.3 You must go to the depth shown to have a perfect parallel squat. *(a)* Back squat, *(b)* front squat.

About halfway up, you pass through the sticking point, the position at which the squat becomes easier. When you reach the sticking point, you should breathe out. Lifters on a heavy squat will sometimes let out a yell as they expel the air in their lungs. This is perfectly acceptable and probably helps with the overall psych of the lift.

Sometimes, especially with a heavy weight, your hips may come up all right but you will lean over. To correct this position, you can try two techniques. First, scoot your hips forward and try to get them underneath the bar. Obviously, you should reexamine our previous technique guidelines for the chest and lower back. The second technique that works extremely well with many athletes is to think "elbows forward." When you press your elbows forward during a squat, you will tend to have an upright torso with a big chest and a locked-in lower back. The hips will follow the elbows. Your eyes should remain fixed on the same point throughout the entire upward drive. When you complete the set, take short, controlled steps back to the rack. Always remain in a solid position as you rack the bar.

PROBLEMS IN SQUATTING

In teaching the squat, I've found two common mistakes—knees in and knees forward. The knees-in problem is more difficult to correct and puts unwanted pressure on the medial collateral ligaments. This problem is quite common among female athletes and boys of junior high age. When squatting, the knees-in problem will surface on the way up. The knees are usually all right on the way down when squatting. The first step is for the coach to yell, "Knees!" to the athlete who is squatting. This is a signal for the athlete to force the knees out over the toes.

This signal may not work the first time. If it doesn't, a second correction technique is to tap the inside of the athlete's knee lightly. This gives the athlete a kinesthetic feel of the problem. The cure usually happens after only a few light taps. If the problem persists, coaches should videotape their athletes performing squats so that they can see themselves. This usually does the trick in those few extreme cases.

The knees-forward problem often occurs with beginners who lift their heels off the ground during the descent. This error puts harmful stress on the patella area, besides causing the lift to be horribly ineffective. Coaches can correct the knees-forward problem by letting the athlete hold on to a partner's hands for balance. The athlete should sit tall, spread the chest, and keep the elbows and shoulders back. The athlete will then be able to balance with the heels on the ground from a parallel-squat position. The partner should let go after a while to let the athlete have a chance to regain balance from that difficult position. Surprisingly, most high school athletes can balance themselves after they get the feel of the parallel position with their heels on the ground.

Most bodybuilders squat with the knees forward and the bar positioned high on the neck. They usually lift with a lighter weight and higher reps and therefore may never have a problem. Athletes, however, usually bring the bar back more on the shoulders and want to lift a lot more weight. If the knees continue to come forward with heavier weights, it is my opinion that this is a potentially dangerous situation. The athlete must attempt to sit back more on the hips, with the lower leg being more vertical.

SPOTTING

Correct spotting technique is critical to proper execution of the squat. Coaches have the responsibility to teach correct spotting techniques. Three spotters—a back spotter and two side spotters—should be used to ensure success in squatting. The functions of the spotters are threefold. First, the spotters should act as coaches and give correct technique cues. Second, they should act as judges on depth and technique problems. Third, they should be enthusiastic teammates and offer constant encouragement. Spotters should pull the best from their training partners.

Figure 6.4 shows correct spotting positions for the parallel squat. The same positions should be used on a front squat. The side spotters are in the correct position for their dual role as coaches and judges. All spotters should know the six absolutes for coaching perfect technique. Spotters need to be vocal in letting their teammate know how he or she is doing. No lifter can see or hear a nod of the head.

Notice the position of the side spotters in figure 6.4. One spotter has his head behind the bar, and the other has his head in front. Spotters must get into these positions to judge the parallel squat. The side spotters need to focus on the top part of the lifter's thigh. They should use the marble test. Which way would a marble roll from the middle of the lifter's thigh? If the marble would roll toward the lifter's knee, the lifter needs to go lower. If the marble would stay stationary or roll toward the lifter's hip, the lift counts. Side spotters need to tell the lifter on every rep whether the lift is good or not good in a voice loud enough for the lifter to understand. Good judges do not count bad reps. Spotters should encourage their teammate during and immediately after the set by offering comments such as "Looking good," "Great job," "Awesome set," "One more rep," or "You can do it." A great set deserves a high five.

Figure 6.4 Example of squat using the 6 Absolutes. Note: the spotters are in perfect position.

The back spotter should place his or her hands firmly on the bar at all times, from the moment the lifter gets under the bar to back out to when he or she puts the bar back on the rack after squatting. The back spotter places his or her hands on the bar for two reasons. First, the spotter can easily correct technique, especially when the lifter leans forward. The back spotter just pulls back slightly but firmly to correct the poor position. In addition, the back spotter should talk and encourage the lifter through the lift and set. Sometimes power lifters spot from behind with the arms going under the lifter's armpits to the chest, but this assumes that technique problems are absent.

The side spotters should be in squat position on the sides with their hands underneath the bar. If something happens, it usually happens quickly, and the spotters need to be ready. Spotters cannot stand on the sides with their arms crossed. The side spotters also should yell something on each rep of every heavy set. Here are some suggestions: "One inch high," "A little lower," "Perfect," "Looking good," "Stay tight," "Eyes," "Fight it," "Be fierce," "One more rep," "Too low," "Spread the chest." After the lifter completes the set, the side spotters grasp the bar and help the lifter back to the rack. I tell the side spotters to put their noses on the rack. If they remain on the side, they just can't see the rack.

BOX SQUAT

For developing hip strength, the box squat is superior to any other free-weight exercise or machine. When we have a chance to demonstrate the box squat at clinics, we always get the same reaction from coaches. They really like this lift because it duplicates the hip movement used in the power sports (football, volleyball, basketball, baseball, and so on). After our demonstrations, we often hear coaches say, "That's what I want! That's what I want!"

I came across the box squat 35 years ago while training in Los Angeles with the world's greatest power lifters and track athletes (shot-putters, discus throwers, and hammer throwers). Los Angeles at that time was the mecca for amateur power athletes. I'd coach high school track, football, and wrestling and then train in Los Angeles with men like George Frenn and Jon Cole.

George Frenn taught me how to box squat. George squatted 853 pounds in competition and won the national hammer-throw championship three years in a row. That 853-pound squat was the best achieved by anybody in the world for years, even though George weighed only 242 pounds. George would box squat once a week and parallel squat once a week. Doing regular squats twice a week was too draining, and George found that he couldn't throw as well in meets or practice. Doing box squats left him with energy for the next day.

Athletes who expect to stay on top of their game need to do sprints and plyometrics and develop the technique of their sport. That routine requires a great deal of time and energy. The box squat allows an athlete to perform a squatting exercise twice a week and still have time and energy to develop athletic abilities. In addition, by adapting to a heavier weight the athlete gains confidence for regular squats.

To perform the box squat, first assume an athletic stance and squat down carefully under control on a box or a high bench. Take care not to plop down out of control because doing so could cause injury. Then settle back (rock back) slightly, making certain that your lower back remains concave in a locked-in position. You then drive forward and up. If you just go down and touch the box or bench, as most athletes do when they perform this exercise, you will develop only the quadriceps. That would be a serious mistake. The final point concerning technique is that you should drive up on your toes in an explosive action as you complete the lift. At this final stage you should have the same feeling you do when blocking, tackling, rebounding, or releasing a track implement (see figure 6.5).

We have always cautioned that plopping down hard on the box can be dangerous to the lower back. You must keep the lower back in tight

Figure 6.5 Correct three-person spotting for the parallel-to-box squat.

and sit down under control. You want to increase the weight you lift on the box squat compared with what you lift on the parallel squat, but you must limit the increase to 100 to 150 pounds. Some athletes make a huge mistake by using 200 to 300 pounds more on the box squat. If you are using the BFS set-rep system, you may want to set a limit of 100 pounds. For example, if your max is 325 pounds on the parallel squat, do not lift any more than 425 pounds on the box squat on one or more reps. Sometimes it gets a bit scary spotting an athlete who is shaking and wobbling all over the place with a huge box squat.

The 100-pound rule keeps things safer and enables you to keep progressing. Other benefits include greater availability of intensity on parallel-squat days. The progress you make on parallel squats will optimize your ability to break box-squat records. The recovery on box-squat day will also be easier and more complete. This cycle of advantages will help you make regular progress and keep your motivation high.

FRONT SQUAT

The front squat is an excellent variation of the parallel squat, because it can help an athlete stay upright and keep the lower back in the correct position.

Figure 6.6 The front squat using the clean grip. This exercise helps develop the lower quadriceps.

Front squats also accentuate development in the lower quadriceps of the thigh, particularly the teardrop-shaped muscle on the inside of the thigh known as the vastus medialis. The vastus medialis is important in preventing knee injuries because it helps the kneecap track properly (figure 6.6).

With front squats, athletes use less weight than they do with back squats. When an athlete reaches the BFS all-state level in the squat or is having trouble maintaining correct form in the back squat, he or she may wish to switch to front squats.

Front squats may be performed several ways. Athletes may hold the barbell as they do in the power clean, with elbows up and forward and resting the bar on the deltoids, or they may cross their arms and hold the bar on the deltoids to give additional support by the upper arms. The easiest and best way for beginners to do the front squat is to use a shoulder-support device such as the Sting Ray™ (figure 6.7).

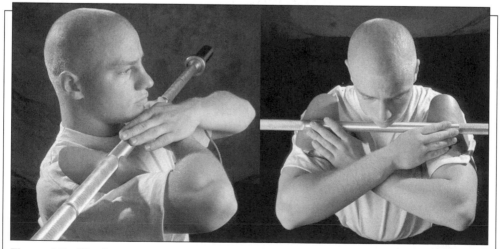

Figure 6.7 The front squat with arms crossed and using a Sting Ray™ device.

SQUAT VARIATIONS

Other acceptable squat variations are the high-bar bodybuilding, or Olympic-style, squat, the safe-bar squat, and the hip sled. In the high-bar bodybuilding squat, athletes use less weight than they do in the parallel squat, and some athletes who choose this option go several inches below parallel. I personally do not like this variation but recognize its acceptability for those who perform it with good technique.

The hip sled is mounted on incline rails and has padded steel appendages for the shoulders and a footplate at the bottom (figure 6.8). The athlete enters the machine facedown and places the shoulders between the appendages and the feet shoulder-width apart on the footplate. Keeping the back arched, the athlete straightens the legs to perform the movement. Because relatively little stability is required to perform this exercise and because the sled is placed at an incline, the athlete can often use more weight on this exercise than he or she does on the box squat. Care must be taken not to bounce the weight out of the bottom position to use more weight, because doing so can place adverse stress on the lower back and knees (see figure 6.9).

Figure 6.8 Hip sled.

Figure 6.9 Squat thrust using hip sled.

LIFTING CHAINS

Lifting chains may be used in the squat and all its variations. Applying the concept of variable resistance, lifting chains gradually make the bar heavier as the athlete lifts the weight so that the muscles work hard during the entire lift. As such, a squat with chains can serve as a substitute for the box squat (see figure 6.10). Normally, adding about 10 percent at the finish position of the lift is most beneficial. I recommend recording what is on the bar plus the weight of the chain that the athlete is lifting.

Those are the basics of productive squatting. If you follow the guidelines closely, you'll develop unbelievably strong quads, glutes, and hamstrings, a combination that translates into reduced susceptibility to injury, improved power, and greater athletic performance.

Figure 6.10 Lifting chains can be used in all variations of the squat.

Power Clean and Quick Lifts

The power clean is of vital importance to athletes. To develop athletic competence, athletes must perform one or more quick lifts such as cleans, snatches, and reverse-grip cleans. Quick lifts can be performed with a squat style (dropping into a full squat when the weight is racked to the shoulders) or a power style (in which there is only a slight bend in the knees). The power clean is the most popular quick lift, and because we base our BFS standards on it, we recommend it first. The power clean develops explosiveness and aggressiveness. Every muscle comes into play, and when done correctly every muscle fires in proper sequence. This summation of forces creates maximum power.

Bruno Pauletto, a former strength coach for the University of Tennessee, wrote a series of articles for our *BFS* magazine. Coach Pauletto described the power clean as "an explosive lift in which speed is a very big factor. With speed being important and heavy weights being moved, the power output is great. The power clean just cannot be done slowly. Other lifts, like the bench and squat, have minimal power output because speed is not a factor; they basically develop strength. Many coaches still believe that the weight room is the place to develop only strength and the field is the place to develop speed. I believe that some lifting exercises go beyond the strength factor and one of them is the power clean."

POWER CLEAN AND ATHLETICS

Because of the way it is performed, the power clean is similar to many athletic movements. The similarities include rotary hip movement, the prestretch, and multijoint movements.

■ **Rotary hip movement.** A biomechanical analysis shows that the rotary action of the legs and hips (that is, the hips moving forward and down) in the power clean is similar to the jumping, running, and pulling actions common to many sports. All such movements require the use of a combined leg and hip drive so that the large, powerful muscles of the legs and hips can bring the hips forward and up. When an athlete performs the power clean, the hips and legs must get underneath the body to push the weight up and out. That action simulates the pushing action in sports, whether it is straight up (as in the high jump) or at an angle (as in tackling). In the power clean the legs and hips move under the body with a rotary action to drive the body to full extension.

■ **Prestretch.** In the middle of the pull when the hips are under the bar, the thighs are positioned so that a stretch, known also as a prestretch, is placed upon them. This prestretch is similar to a plyometric jump, and it enables the muscles of the legs to contract more forcefully. As athletes perfect this phase of the lift, their muscles will react more explosively.

■ **Multijoint movement.** The power clean is a complete lift because so many muscle groups work when performing the exercise. This multijoint exercise works the ankles, knees, hips, back, shoulders, elbows, wrists, and most of the muscles associated with those joints. Muscle coordination improves because the muscles work together in a chain reaction. For a powerful total-body movement to occur, each joint and the associated muscles must produce proper force at the right time. When these forces work together, the result is a force of great magnitude. The power clean is one of a few resistance exercises that can produce this great force.

Power cleans develop explosive power, especially in a marginal athlete. Football coaches are often puzzled by the player with a big upper body who just can't hit. Conversely, they are amazed by the 155-pound player who just knocks his opponents' socks off. The clean can help athletes who do not have natural hitting ability. To help athletes develop their potential, we have set certain standards. The varsity high school standard for males is 175 pounds, for all-state it's 235 pounds, and for all-American it's 300 pounds. Changes really start to happen when athletes reach the 200-pound level because at that level they must execute the lift with correct technique and quickness.

I saw a dramatic example of the benefits of the power clean when I worked with Mark Eaton of the Utah Jazz. When he was cleaning only 115 pounds, he would wimp it up, and that's how he looked when rebounding and when blocking shots. But as his technique improved, he developed a much more aggressive attitude toward the clean. Later, he cleaned 250 pounds and would let out a roar and explode through the lift. Mark led the NBA in blocked shots and was an NBA all-star in 1989. He made so much progress that I wanted to put a football helmet on him.

I believe that the clean is a safe lift. In fact, many more injuries are attributed to the bench press than to the clean. At BFS we know more than anyone else does about what is happening with athletic programs around the country. We keep in touch with tens of thousands of athletes and coaches in every corner of the United States. At this point, we just do not have anybody complaining about the clean. I do not want to recommend something dangerous. Cleans are safe!

Safety is always our most important consideration. Here are the BFS technique guidelines, which will greatly reduce the possibility of injury and increase your chances of success:

All-Star Mark Eaton used the BFS power clean program, increasing his strength and explosiveness to become one of the best shot-blockers in the NBA.

General Principles

To perform the clean safely, athletes must follow these general guidelines:

■ Never perform more than five reps during a set.

■ Power clean with heavy weight only once a week.

■ Do not bounce the bar on the floor between reps.

1. Start with your back in a concave position. Spread your chest. Your feet should be flat on the floor, especially the heels. Place your shins on the line on the bar where the knurling begins (figure 7.1).

2. Get into a jump stance. Your arms should be straight. When the bar is touching your shins, feel the steel. Make sure that you position your hands on the bar very close to your legs (figure 7.2).

3. As you begin to pull, make sure that your chin is up. Keep your shoulders close to your ears (figure 7.3) and your elbows high. Think "elbows to the ceiling" (figure 7.4). Keep the bar as close to your chest as possible.

4. Start the upward movement in a slow, controlled pull. Never jerk the bar from the floor. After the bar passes your knees, jump straight up as explosively as you can (figure 7.4).

Figure 7.1   Start position for the power clean.

5. Pull the bar high and snap explosively under the bar, with your elbows snapping forward under the bar. Your feet should pop out into an athletic stance. As your body surges under the bar, your lower back should be in a concave position (figure 7.5).

Figure 7.2 Jump stance.

Figure 7.3 Shoulder shrug.

Figure 7.4 Elbows to the ceiling.

Figure 7.5 Catch position.

The most effective coaching point I've found while doing clinics is to yell "Jump!" when the lifter takes the bar just past the knees. I can talk about double dipping or using the thighs or ramming the hips forward, but nothing works like yelling "Jump!" When an athlete jumps at the right time, the effect is good technique at a crucial part of this important lift.

The clean is one of the most popular lifts among strength coaches. I estimate that about 90 percent of strength coaches use the clean movement for a basic power-building exercise. I strongly recommend the clean. It is a valuable lift for football, basketball, track, baseball, and all sports dealing with explosive power.

Hang Clean

The hang clean requires the same type of explosive movement as the power clean does. You might choose the hang clean to replace the power clean as a core lift for two reasons. First, you may want to switch exercises every three to six months for variation to help overcome plateaus. Second, performed correctly, the hang clean is less stressful to the lower back. If you have previously injured your lower back or have chronic lower-back problems, you may be able to perform the hang clean without aggravation.

The technique of the hang clean is virtually the same as that used for the power clean. Begin the hang clean in the erect position with the bar resting on the middle of the thighs. Now dip down to the middle pull position, with your shoulders slightly in front of the bar, and then immediately begin the explosive jump phase. The technique from this point on is the same as the technique used for the power clean.

Power Snatch and Hang Power Snatch

As with the power clean and the hang clean, the power snatch and the hang power snatch require an explosive jump phase. Many athletes prefer a snatching movement, because it can be easier on the wrists, elbows, and shoulders than the movements in the clean variations are. Normally, athletes can power snatch between 70 and 75 percent of the weight they use in the power clean.

The technique of the power snatch is the same as that used for the power clean, except that athletes use a wide grip and whip the bar overhead to arms' length rather than catch it on the shoulders (figure 7.6).

Figure 7.6 The power snatch.

Hex-Bar Deadlift and Deadlift Variations

In the early years of BFS, athletes performed both the deadlift and the power clean on the same day. As the BFS program evolved, we decided to replace the deadlift with the hex-bar deadlift, an exercise performed with a hexagonal barbell that weighs 45 pounds. The hexagonal shape allows the lifter to perform exercises from inside the encompassing bar. Handgrips strategically placed on the two ends of the bar enable the weight on the bar to be in perfect alignment with the power line at all times. Figure 8.1a-c illustrates the unique aspects of the hex bar.

The power line is an imaginary line that runs straight up through the lifter's center mass. Executing the deadlift movement through the power line enables the athlete to develop maximum power and reduces risk of injury. The farther the weight diverges from the power line, the more power the lifter loses. For example, how long can you hold a 45-pound bar with your arms straight down and the bar resting against your thighs? Probably for a long time. Now try holding the bar about a foot out from your thighs. Doing that is much harder. The farther away the bar gets from center mass, the harder it is to hold, and the more power is lost. In addition, because the hex bar makes using correct technique easy, a spotter is not necessary.

The hex-bar deadlift strengthens the lower back, hamstrings, thighs, torso, and traps. Although the deadlift can still be used in the BFS program as an auxiliary lift, we've found the hex-bar deadlift a superior

Figure 8.1 The hex-bar deadlift, *(a* and *c)* places less stress on the lower back compared to the straight bar *(b)* because the weight is closer to the hips.

exercise. Because the torso is more upright than it is with the regular deadlift, compression forces on the spine and stress on the lower back are reduced. This difference makes it possible for athletes to work the lower back hard every week, whereas such frequency of training with the regular deadlift often causes overtraining. The hex bar also lends itself to doing shrugs in a superior way because the bar does not contact the thighs. Dave Williams, the strength coach at Liberty University, says, "The hex bar is a tremendous training tool."

The hex bar is a space saver. It is only 56 inches long, compared with the 86 inches of space that regular Olympic bars occupy. This compactness allows placement of many hex-bar stations in a small area. In addition, the shorter length of the bar decreases the distance of the weight from the lifter, giving the lifter more control and balance for a more efficient, higher intensity workout.

Hex-bar workouts are also fast. On one of my first workouts with the hex bar, I did five sets of five reps, going up to 375 pounds. The workout took much less time than a squat or deadlift workout would—only eight minutes. I was extremely sore the next day in my glutes, hamstrings, and traps. I could hardly walk. The workout was just like a heavy parallel-squat workout when I hadn't squatted for a while, but my lower back felt great. I was impressed.

NO-FEAR DEADLIFT

Conquering the fear of the deadlift is the purpose of using the hex bar! The deadlift is a superb exercise for the lower body and torso, but for years fear has overshadowed the great benefits of the deadlift. Coaches and athletes have been afraid of the heavy weight and difficult technique associated with the deadlift. The key to conquering this fear is proper technique. As with all lifts, proper technique will eliminate potential injury. With the hex bar, executing great technique has never been easier. The hex bar makes doing the deadlift easy and fun for anyone.

To perform the deadlift with the hex or high hex bar, the lifter steps into the center of the hexagon and assumes the jump stance. The lifter then squats down and grabs the handgrips on both sides of the bar, making sure to place the hands squarely in the middle of the handles for balance. The lifter lowers the hips, spreads the chest, locks the lower back in place, keeps the head up with the eyes forward, and puts the knees directly over the feet. The lifter then lifts the bar straight up through the power line using the legs.

Because of the unique design of the hex bar, the lifter can keep the weight along the power line throughout the entire lift. Once the lifter has stood up completely, the first repetition is complete and the lifter is ready for the next rep. The lifter should proceed to squat back down, again keeping the lower back locked in, the chest spread, and the eyes on target. To minimize back strain, the athlete should bounce the weights slightly off the floor when doing repetitions. Pausing in the down position after each rep is not necessary or desirable. As in all lifts, the head should be up and the chin stretched away from the chest. If the chin touches the chest, the entire body will become dangerously out of position. That technique reduces the amount of weight that the athlete can lift and, more important, is dangerous and can cause injury to the lower back.

A variation of the hex bar is the high hex bar. They are identical except that the high hex bar has elevated handgrips. The higher starting position allowed by the high hex bar makes executing exercises easier for beginning lifters and tall lifters. The high hex bar also provides an excellent way to add variety to workouts.

STRAIGHT-LEG DEADLIFT

The BFS straight-leg deadlift is a high-priority auxiliary lift. We think of this lift as a stretching exercise. Therefore, our recommended technique is to use a very light weight and do every rep slowly, controlled, and deep. Junior high boys and girls should use 45 pounds or less. Most high school female athletes should use between 45 and 65 pounds. Very strong, mature female high school athletes could use up to a maximum of 95 pounds. Very strong, mature male high school athletes could use up to a maximum of 135 pounds. The absolute max anyone should use is 40 percent of their parallel squat. Do two sets of ten repetitions two times per week, and do not try to do a little more each week. Keep the poundage the same.

Begin the straight-leg dead lift with a very slow and controlled movement. Keep your legs straight with the knees locked (not hyperextended) at all times (see figure 8.2). When you do a hamstring stretch, you can't bend the knee at all; same thing with the BFS straight-leg deadlift. You can pause at the bottom before coming back up. To get a deeper stretch, perform the lift while standing on a low platform (see figure 8.3).

SPOTTED DEADLIFT

Once or twice a year it's a great idea to put on an event for your team featuring the deadlift with a spotter, especially with football players. The coach and all team members should have a wild max-out party. Everyone shouts, "Go-go-go!" as each team member has a turn. This kind of event can generate awesome intensity. We do this at BFS clinics, and the average high school football player can lift 400 pounds. Our all-state standard is 500 pounds, and the all-American standard is 600 pounds.

In power-lifting contests, of course, athletes cannot use a spotter for the deadlift. For schools that keep records of weights for the deadlift, I recommend establishing records from reps in which a spotter is not used. A spotter usually assists by lifting 50 to 75 pounds, a contribution that would invalidate an athlete's record. During regular training, using a

Figure 8.2 Straight-leg deadlift on floor.

Figure 8.3 Straight-leg deadlift on platform for a deeper stretch.

spotter is vital for safety. With sufficient training, athletes will be ready to lift unassisted when it's time for contests and setting records.

With the spotted deadlift, the spotter presses down with one hand on the lower back and hooks the other around the lifter's shoulder and chest. The spotter secures the crook of the elbow against the shoulder and places the fist or hand firmly in the middle of the chest. The spotter and lifter should coordinate the lift, perhaps by having the spotter say, "One-two-up."

As the lift begins, the spotter pulls up and back while pushing in on the lower back (see figure 8.4). This technique is important for safety. The spotter pulls back to get the weight back on the lifter's heels. When high school athletes deadlift by themselves, the weight often shifts toward the toes. This shift not only reduces the amount of weight lifted but also can injure the lower back. When the weight shifts back toward the heels, athletes can normally deadlift in complete safety.

As with all BFS core lifts, keeping records and setting goals is important. For male athletes, the BFS varsity standard for the hex-bar deadlift or spotted deadlift is 400 pounds, the all-state standard is 500 pounds, and the all-American standard is 600 pounds. Female athletes have a varsity standard of 235 pounds, an all-state standard of 325 pounds, and an all-American standard of 415 pounds.

Now let's go set some records!

Figure 8.4 Proper positions for the spotted deadlift.

Taylor Twins—Twice the Talent

Weight training is key for Brenda and Lindsay Taylor.

Imagine a beautiful teenage girl who grows up to earn an academic scholarship at an Ivy League school and, while there, establishes herself as one of the best collegiate track and field athletes in the country. After graduating with a degree in one of the most difficult majors, such as mechanical engineering or perhaps cognitive neuroscience, she goes on to become a contender for an Olympic gold medal. Considering the difficulty of achieving this level of success in both athletics and academics, you might say that it's possible, but not probable, that such a woman could exist. Now imagine that there are identical twins who have achieved exactly that. Sound too far-fetched? Then you should meet Brenda and Lindsay Taylor.

In the world of track and field, there has never been anything quite like Brenda and Lindsay Taylor. Identical twins from Boone, North Carolina, these 23-year-old women have established themselves as athletes who have excellent chances of making the next Olympic team.

Brenda, an outstanding hurdler, won the 2001 NCAA Track and Field Championships in the 400-meter hurdles, placed third at the U.S. Nationals and made the semifinals of the World Championships. She also received the Honda Award as America's top collegiate female athlete in track and field. This year she placed third at the U.S. Nationals (she did not compete in the World Championships in 2002, as they are held every two years). Brenda's best time is 55.46 seconds.

Lindsay, a heptathlete, was also a standout in college, earning 11 Ivy League titles and breaking seven school records. She placed sixth in 2003 in the U.S. Nationals. Her best score is 5,578. Impressive physical accomplishments, don't you agree?

Despite having the opportunity to attend any major college on their athletic scholarships, the twins decided to accept academic scholarships to Ivy League universities. Brenda, who plans to become a doctor, graduated from Harvard with a degree in cognitive neuroscience. Lindsay graduated from

Brown University with a degree in mechanical engineering and a minor in biomedical engineering and plans on pursuing a PhD.

The twins were gymnasts from the age of six, but their height became an issue because they, as Brenda says, "started breaking equipment." Next on the list was swimming, followed by volleyball, which they participated in throughout high school, and then track and field. "We didn't start track until our freshman year in high school," says Brenda. "We were decent swimmers and volleyball players, but we were much more successful in track. When the time came that colleges were recruiting, they were calling me about track and not about swimming. And both of us liked track much better."

Because they were such great athletes, Joel Williams, the track coach at Watauga High School, decided to put the twins in as many events as possible. Brenda comments, "In high school Lindsay and I were on the same team. To score as many points as possible we would be put into different events. So instead of having us come in first and second, I was put into events where I could get first and Lindsay was put into events where she could get first. I was a stronger sprinter and hurdler than Lindsay, and Lindsay was a stronger jumper, so she would focus on the jumps and I would focus on the sprints and hurdles."

A key part of the Taylor twins' conditioning is weight training, which they took up seriously in high school. Lindsay says, "When I was in high school the football coach was an avid reader of *BFS* magazine, and his weight training program was a product of what he had read. He helped my high school track coach work out a program based on what he had learned from BFS." At present, both women have progressed to the level where they can power clean 190 pounds; Lindsay can full squat 250, whereas Brenda can full squat 280 and parallel squat 350.

Although many superstar athletes would argue that academics interferes with their training, Lindsay says that the discipline that track and field develops, especially in regard to time management, can carry over to other aspects of life. "With the discipline it takes to be successful in our sport, you find that track athletes tend to excel in any other areas they put their minds to. For some it may be the classroom, and for others it may be their job." Brenda agrees: "Athletes must structure their time really well, so they learn how to be disciplined in just about everything they do."

Bench Press and Bench-Press Variations

Just as the squat is the king of lower-body exercises, the bench press is at the top for its ability to develop overall strength in the upper body—the chest, shoulders, and triceps. Although some strength coaches choose to leave it out of their programs, I believe that the bench press is essential.

For one thing, the standards are easily recognizable. Athletes want to work harder to achieve the magic standards of 200-, 300-, 400-, or 500-pound benches. Although the value of a 600-pound bench press is questionable, the great male champions of size, strength, and speed seem to have the ability to bench press at least 400 pounds. For female athletes, this exercise is especially important, because they carry proportionately less muscle mass in their upper bodies than males do. This gap in strength often compromises their ability to play sports at a high level. The standards we use for women are 100, 150, 200, and 250 pounds. Thus, if I were a high school coach I would be pleased to see a girl bench press 100 pounds. A bench of 150 pounds is a rare accomplishment for a high school girl, and 200 pounds is a weight few women other than college throwers can lift.

BODY POSITION

Having proper position is extremely important in preventing injury and accidents when lifting. A common fault of novice lifters is keeping the legs straight and taking a leg off the floor during the bench press. This action destroys the firm foundation necessary for maximum effort. Follow these steps to perform the bench press safely and correctly.

1. Start with your body positioned so that the barbell is directly over you eyes. This position provides enough clearance to prevent the bar from hitting the uprights or safety catches as you perform the lift.

2. Spread your legs wide for a solid base and place your feet flat on the floor and under the knees.

3. Then, by placing your hands on the support standards, push your shoulders down toward the hips. An arch should be present in the lower back, with your chest sticking up as high as possible. Although this position is a little uncomfortable, it gives the best mechanical advantage and reduces the possibility that you will illegally arch your hips up from the bench (see figures 9.1, 9.2, and 9.3).

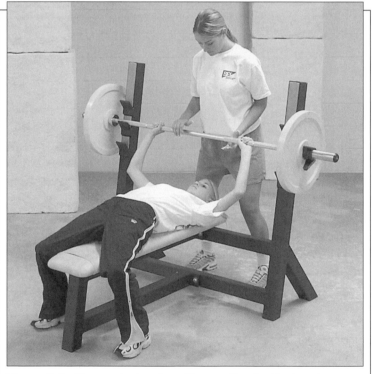

Figure 9.1   Proper start and spotting position for the bench press.

Figure 9.2 Correct lifting and spotting position with the bar on the chest.

Figure 9.3 The spotter must remain alert and help the lifter rack the bar.

Grip

The spacing of the hands affects the position of the elbows and, consequently, affects the muscles and areas that the lift will develop. A close grip forces the elbows in and results in the triceps working more than the chest muscles do. A wider grip allows the elbows to be out away from the body. Most champion bench pressers use a wide grip. With this grip the elbows should be at a right angle when the bar is touching the chest. Female athletes may use a comparably wide grip (figure 9.4), or they may have greater success with a relatively narrow grip (figure 9.5), depending on the structure of their upper bodies.

If I were strictly into power lifting, I'd recommend the wide grip. But few sports, even football and wrestling, involve use of the arms in

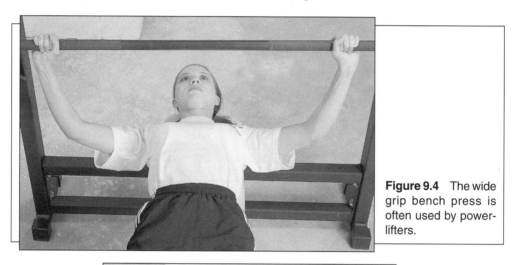

Figure 9.4 The wide grip bench press is often used by power-lifters.

Figure 9.5 The narrow grip bench press emphasizes the triceps.

a wide position. A football player, for example, uses the arms with the elbows in close. Therefore, I recommend a narrower grip with the elbows in on the bench press to simulate the action that a defensive lineman, linebacker, or a bottom-positioned wrestler uses. In 1979 the Pittsburgh Steelers had a group of defensive linemen who could all bench press 450 pounds or more with a narrow, elbows-in grip. (Note that on reaching the halfway point of a narrow-grip bench press, the lifter may force the elbows out for a stronger lockout.)

A word of caution is appropriate here. The bench press is the most dangerous lift in the weight room. For this reason, I strongly recommend placing the thumbs around the bar. Doing otherwise presents too much risk that the bar will slip and drop on the throat or face. I know 10 lifters who have died bench pressing. Many lifters have suffered crushed throats, flattened chins, torn lips, lost teeth, smashed noses, torn eyebrows, loss of sight, scalped hair, and smashed foreheads. Most of these accidents occur at home, nearly all without a spotter present. Keep your thumbs around the bar. Never lift alone. Always use an alert, smart spotter.

Technique

The following paragraphs discuss the proper technique for performing the bench press. In order to get the most out of the lift it's important to follow each of these tips. And remember, always use a spotter for safety.

■ **Breathing.** Take a deep breath in as the bar comes down. Hold your breath just before the bar touches the chest and up to halfway through the upward movement. At that point you can let the breath out forcefully. Some lifters make loud sounds as they force their breath out. This method keeps everything firm and may have some psychological benefit, especially on rep work.

■ **Squeezing the bar.** Before a max attempt, the technique of squeezing the bar very tightly can help—in most cases adding about five pounds. This technique may also reduce stress on the elbows.

■ **Angle.** The bar does not go straight down and straight up, but rather at a slight angle back toward the rack or the lifter's face. As a general guideline, men should lower the barbell to the nipple line, whereas women should lower the barbell to slightly below that level. Finding the correct groove can make a lot of difference in pounds. Some refer to this movement as a C curve.

■ **Focus.** If the bar reaches a sticking point, the lifter can sometimes just look at and concentrate on the right hand to cause the bar to lock out. I often see bench pressers strain with their eyes closed. Taking that approach is a mistake. The eyes should always be open and focused on a point directly overhead.

■ **Spotting.** Most weight-training accidents occur at home without a spotter. I like to use one spotter in the middle when the weight is less than 300 pounds. A single spotter in the middle can provide a more even liftoff and more control over the spot. With heavier poundage, I recommend having two spotters for the liftoff.

Because working out in groups of three or four is preferred anyway, it doesn't hurt to have everyone involved in spotting. The principal spotter assists the lifter from behind at the middle of the bar and lifts the bar from the standards to the lifter. He or she helps the lifter through the sticking point if the athlete has trouble with the weight. The two side spotters should be on opposite ends of the bar. They touch the bar only when the principal spotter calls for help or when the lifter can't lift the bar from the chest.

VARIATIONS

Athletes should perform two bench workouts per week all year round. Benching three times per week will lead to overtraining and overuse injuries such as tendinitis in many athletes. Athletes can make more progress over a long period by benching twice per week.

One of the workouts should be intense, and the other should be different and less intense. Variations in the bench will help athletes achieve new maxes month after month. Our choice for the second workout is the towel bench press. For this variation, the athlete places a thick round cushion (the BFS towel bench pad is five inches in diameter) under the shirt to prevent the barbell from touching the chest. (If a towel bench pad is not available, the athlete can make one with three towels rolled up to about a five-inch diameter. The problem with this approach is getting a consistent thickness of the padding.) The towel bench increases confidence and helps prevent pain or injury to the shoulder-joint area.

Other choices for the second workout could be a combination of wide- and close-grip benches, a light to medium regular bench workout, or a concentration of heavy dips and triceps pushdowns.

Towel Bench Press

I recommend towel benches for three reasons. First, athletes become accustomed to a heavier weight. Normally, on the towel bench athletes can use a weight 10 to 20 pounds heavier than what they use on the regular bench press. Being successful with the heavier weight builds confidence for attaining new levels on the regular bench. Second, the towel bench brings variety to the routine. Variety is important because it helps athletes overcome plateaus. Third, and most important, towel benches go a long way in preventing what I call bench-press shoulder.

Through doing many clinics and talking to many coaches and athletes, we became aware of the problem of bench-press shoulder. We estimate that 75 percent of all athletes who bench press three times per week have it. Specifically, bench-press shoulder is a dull to sharp pain in the front shoulder-joint area where the upper arm, chest, and shoulder meet. This pain comes from working out too often with too much weight. Typically, an athlete with this problem has been doing benches three times a week with maximum or near-maximum poundage. The real stress to the shoulder-joint area comes when the bar is one or two inches from the chest. Stretching and putting stress on the shoulder-joint area three times a week with maximum poundage is bound to cause problems.

To perform a towel bench, place the towel bench pad under your shirt. If you don't have a towel bench pad, take three towels and fold them in half the long way. Place them on top of each other and roll them up like a sleeping bag. Lay the rolled-up towels on your chest and then bench with normal technique (figure 9.6). Bring the bar right into the pad, with more than just a light touch, before driving up.

Figure 9.6 The towel bench press and a perfect spot.

Incline Bench Press

The incline bench press places more emphasis on the shoulders, and the angle from which you press is more specific to many sport movements than the bench press is. Because the pectoral muscles are not as involved, you will press less than you can with a flat bench press. I recommend using a bench that is angled at 45 degrees, making it halfway between a military press and a bench press. Depending on your sport, you may want to use other angles.

Figure 9.7 The incline bench press places more emphasis on the shoulders.

To perform the incline bench press, lie face up on an incline bench-press station. For greatest stability, spread your legs slightly wider than shoulder-width apart and place your feet flat on the floor. As with the regular bench press, grasp the barbell with a shoulder-width grip and have a spotter help you position the weight at arms' length directly above your throat (figure 9.7).

Lower the weight to the upper portion of your pectorals, creating the shortest distance for the bar to travel. As you lower the weight, your elbows should point slightly down, not directly out to your sides. Without bouncing the barbell off your chest, press the weight back to the start, with the barbell traveling in a slight arch backward. At first this action may feel awkward, because the natural tendency is to press the barbell forward, but you'll quickly master the technique. When you've completed all the reps for a set, have your spotter help guide the barbell back to the supports. Breathe using the same technique you used with the flat bench press.

Lifting Chains

Lifting chains can be used in the bench press and all its variations. Applying the concept of variable resistance, lifting chains gradually make the bar heavier as you lift the weight. Your muscles therefore work as hard as possible during the entire lift (see figure 9.8). You can use a bench press with chains as a substitute for the towel bench press. Normally, adding about 10 percent at the finish position of the lift is most beneficial. I recommend recording what is on the bar plus the weight of the chain you are lifting.

To get the most from the bench press and its variations while avoiding injury, always follow our safety protocols and train conservatively. Improper technique and overtraining can quickly undo all the positive effects the bench press has to offer. It is true that you can have too much of a good thing!

Figure 9.8 Lifting chains makes the bar heavier as you lift the weight.

Auxiliary Lifts

Auxiliary lifts receive less emphasis than core lifts do. Athletes perform core lifts in the once-per-month BFS set-rep rotation system, whereas they normally do auxiliary lifts in two sets of 10 reps. An athlete training with a small group performs the auxiliaries after performing the core lifts. With larger groups, coaches rotate their athletes between core lifts and auxiliaries as outlined in chapter 15, "Organization, Weight-Room Design, and Safety."

Select no more than five auxiliary lifts. Performing more than five auxiliary exercises will cause problems, because athletes will not have enough time and energy to do the necessary sprinting, stamina, flexibility, plyometrics, agility, and technique work required for their sport. Think of the total package. You must not overemphasize one area of training at the expense of another. Remember, the ultimate objective is for athletes to reach their potential and *win*. Therefore, select only those exercises that will effectively contribute to the ultimate objective.

Selection of auxiliary lifts depends on choosing those that will help you win or prevent specific injuries. For example, neck exercises are extremely important to football players and wrestlers. But neck exercises are not that important to basketball or baseball players, so you select an auxiliary that *is* important.

Our BFS clinicians rated 100 auxiliary lifts and came up with a list of preferred lifts and a schedule for the days on which athletes should perform them. We have divided these auxiliary lifts into two categories—standard and advanced.

STANDARD AUXILIARY LIFTS

Standard lifts are relatively safe, easy to perform, and require less coaching and lifting expertise than the advanced auxiliaries do. Of course, coaches and athletes must be careful and thoughtful as they do the standard auxiliaries.

The incline press is the only auxiliary that requires a spotter. Most high school and college gyms already have all the equipment necessary to implement these auxiliaries. One exception is the glute-ham machine, which some gyms might not own but which should be a top-priority auxiliary on anyone's list. This lift is also among the BFS advanced auxiliaries. Table 10.1 shows how you can organize the standard auxiliary exercises in your weekly training sessions.

These exercises, with the exception of the neck exercise, fit all sports well. Basketball players, for example, don't need to work on the neck to win in their sport. Therefore, those athletes may leave it out entirely or replace it with another of their choosing. Here are the BFS auxiliary lifts and why they will help you win:

1. Neck exercise. Obviously important in football, wrestling, and soccer. You may use a neck harness, neck machine, or the buddy system (see figure 10.1, page 107).

2. Leg curl. Develops the hamstrings and strengthens the knee-joint area. Helps develop speed and prevent injury (see figure 10.2, page 107).

Table 10.1 Weekly Auxiliary Lifting Schedule

Monday	Wednesday	Friday
Neck exercise	Lat pull	Neck exercise
Leg curl	Heavy dips	Leg curl
Leg extension	Incline press	Leg extension
Glute-ham raise	Shoulder press	Glute-ham raise
Straight-leg deadlift	Lunge	Straight-leg deadlift

Figure 10.1 Neck exercise performed on a seated neck machine.

Figure 10.2
Leg curls develop the hamstrings.

3. Leg extension. Develops the quadriceps and strengthens the knee-joint area. Helps prevent injuries to the knee (see figure 10.3, page 109).

4. Glute-ham raise. A superior way to develop the gluteus maximus, gluteus minimus, and the entire area of the buttocks. The exercise also strengthens the hamstrings, especially in the lower area and specifically from origin to insertion. Helps prevent hamstring pulls (see figure 10.4, page 109).

5. Heavy dips. Unbelievable for developing powerful triceps. Stronger athletes should use a dip belt. When I was doing heavy lifting, I used five 45-pound plates and did five dips. This exercise is fantastic for offensive lineman and defensive football personnel as well as shot-putters. Dips help basketball players with their jump shooting and benefit athletes in all sports that involve throwing an implement or ball (see figure 10.5, page 110).

6. Incline press. A favorite auxiliary lift for many athletes. The lift develops the upper-chest area and aids the bench press. It duplicates shot putting and an offensive lineman's pass-blocking position (see figure 10.6, page 110).

7. Lunge. Develops power balance. Each leg must work independently of the other. In addition, the exercise puts no stress on the lower back. Athletes may do this exercise with dumbbells or a regular bar. It develops the hamstrings, quadriceps, and buttocks (see figure 10.7, page 111).

8. Straight-leg deadlift. Athletes should think of this auxiliary as a stretching exercise. They should use very light weight and do each rep in a slow, controlled manner. Most athletes should use between 55 and 135 pounds. Beginning high school athletes should start with no more than 55 pounds. They do not try to break records on this lift. Stretching the hamstrings is the goal. They do this exercise for speed. The exercise is magic because it stretches and strengthens the glutes and hamstrings at the same time (see figure 10.8, page 111).

9. Lat pull. The most common way to do lat pulls is to use a wide grip and pull the bar down behind the neck. But many strength coaches have recently recommended doing the pulling movement in front of the neck rather than behind it to reduce risk of injury. Athletes can use other methods on certain lat-pull machines by using the various grips that are provided (see figure 10.9, page 112).

10. Shoulder press. Athletes using both shoulder-press machines and free-weight benches use a two-hand press. They can also do shoulder presses with dumbbells, alternating the right and left arms, and with a quarter turn to the inside on the way up. The latest research indicates that doing behind-the-neck shoulder presses are not as effective. Therefore, we recommend doing shoulder-press movements in front (see figure 10.10, page 112).

Figure 10.3 Leg extensions develop the quadriceps and strengthen the knee joints.

Figure 10.4 The glute-ham raise helps prevent hamstring pulls.

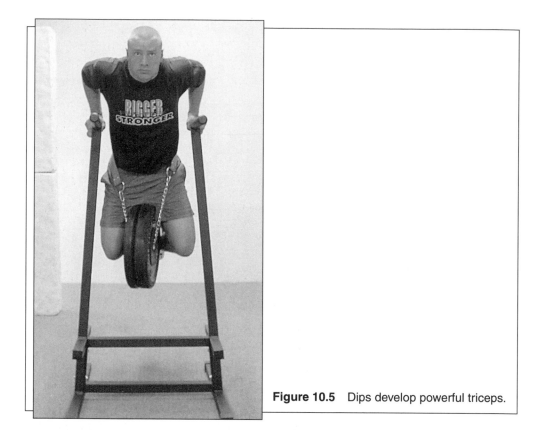

Figure 10.5 Dips develop powerful triceps.

Figure 10.6
The incline press.

Figure 10.7
The lunge, which can also be performed by holding dumbbells.

Figure 10.8
The straight-leg deadlift stretches and strengthens the glutes.

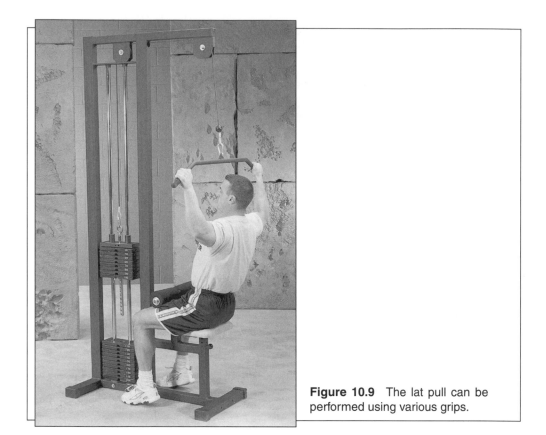

Figure 10.9 The lat pull can be performed using various grips.

Figure 10.10 Shoulder presses can be performed seated, standing, and with dumbbells.

Another auxiliary exercise that may be valuable to athletes, especially those who are rehabilitating injuries, is the leg press. For athletes not able to perform the squat or hip sled, the leg press is a good alternative. Leg-press machines come in many variations, but the most popular positions places the athlete at a 45-degree incline from which he or she pushes a sled upward.

ADVANCED AUXILIARY LIFTS

The advanced auxiliary lifts are harder to perform than BFS standard auxiliaries and require more coaching and organization. Any overhead lift is considered an advanced lift. Coaches should use caution before giving the green light for larger groups. Only after learning the basic lifting techniques, such as the six absolutes, will athletes benefit from these exercises. These lifts include the power snatch, jerk, push jerk, and the balance drills.

■ **Power snatch.** The power snatch is a tremendous lift for any athlete and not all that hard to perform. Many athletes find this exercise easier on the wrists than the power clean. If you can perform a power clean with good technique, you might want to try a power snatch. Perform two sets of five reps. You can even use the power snatch as a core lift. See chapter 7 for more information on this exercise.

■ **Push jerk.** Place the barbell behind the neck in a high-bar squat position, squat down slightly, and thrust the bar explosively upward. As you do this, quickly spread your feet apart as you would when doing an Olympic-style clean and jerk. The bar will end up overhead in a locked position, at which point you stand upright to complete the lift (see figure 10.11, page 114). Do two sets of five reps. Jerk presses develop upper-body explosiveness and shoulder strength. You can also perform this exercise with the barbell resting on the front of the shoulders, using the starting position of the shoulder press.

■ **Push press.** Assume the position you used for the jerk press and squat down slightly. Thrust the bar upward explosively with the legs and arms. Then explosively pop your feet out from your jump stance into a high squat position as you do in a power clean. Do two sets of five reps.

■ **Power balance drills.** You can perform these challenging and entertaining drills in tandem with the power snatch. The neat thing about our balance drills is that using only the bar they can challenge even a strong athlete.

Figure 10.11   The push jerk.

POWER BALANCE AUXILIARY DRILLS

I have used the term *power balance* for many years. In the past at BFS, lunges have been the primary auxiliary exercise used to develop power balance. Exercises that demand balance use stabilizing muscles about as much as they use the prime movers. Free weights normally develop the stabilizing muscles more than machines do.

In simple terms, when balance comes into play during exercise, the body uses many different muscles. This factor is one of the primary reasons that athletes choose free weights over machines. For example, the prime movers in a standing-curl exercise are the biceps, but were it not for the stabilizing muscles in the back and hips, the lifter would fall over. I want athletes to stride out a long way during lunges, thereby learning to balance themselves powerfully in an awkward position, a position many times duplicated in athletic competition.

Tom Cross, who has been a strength coach at Mid-American Nazarene College, caused me to think about some additional power balance lifts several years ago. As a result, I began including three of these during my auxiliary lift presentation at BFS clinics. Before I give this lift presentation, the athletes and coaches have experienced a thorough practical introduction to the six absolutes of coaching and have worked on the power clean for about an hour. During the power-clean presentation, all athletes have experienced a front squat from a power-clean position. The final lift I present at a BFS clinic before I discuss the three power balance lifts is the power snatch. I offer this background because I recommend that all athletes go through the same experience before trying the following three power balance lifts.

I have 10 stations set up with BFS training plates, so most athletes are successful with a power snatch at a clinic. If they can do a power snatch, they are ready for an entertaining challenge such as the power balance drills.

1. **Power balance drill #1.** Perform a power snatch and stand erect in an athletic stance. Now squat all the way down while maintaining great balance and technique. Hold the low position for three seconds and then stand erect again (figure 10.12a).

2. **Power balance drill #2.** Place the bar on your shoulders as if you are going to do a back squat while using a snatch grip. Again, squat all the way down and balance yourself. Then see if you can press the weight all the way up. The challenge is to see if you can press the bar up from your shoulders while maintaining perfect balance (figure 10.12b).

3. **Power balance drill #3.** Do power balance drill #2 but this time see if you can press it up, hold it for three seconds, and then stand erect (figure 10.12c).

Variation helps keep athletes motivated so that they continue to train hard and break records. Coaches should have their athletes focus on the core lifts but use these auxiliary lifts to ensure greater commitment to success.

Figure 10.12 Key positions for *(a)* power balance drill #1, *(b)* power balance drill #2, and *(c)* power balance drill #3.

PART III

Speed, Agility, and Flexibility

Agility and the BFS Dot Drill

To train harder and prevent muscle pulls, athletes need to work up a little sweat and increase their body temperature before sprinting, stretching, or lifting heavy weights. Some athletes perform aerobic exercises such as jogging to warm up, but these activities do little to improve athletic ability. The BFS dot drill is the perfect warm-up for athletes because it develops agility. What's more, it's challenging, fun, and takes only a minute.

Place five dots on the floor (figure 11.1). The drill works best with four-inch dots painted on the floor. Some coaches paint many stations for larger groups. At home, athletes can use anything approved by their parents to mark the dots. There are five components to the dot drill. Athletes perform each drill six times.

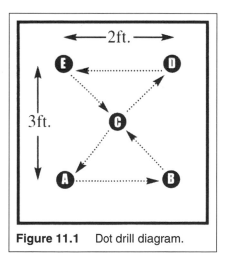

Figure 11.1   Dot drill diagram.

1. Up and Back

1. Start at one end with feet on A and B (left foot on A, right foot on B).

2. Jump quickly with both feet to C, then with split feet to D and E.

3. Come back the same way, without turning around.

4. Repeat five times.

2. Right Foot

1. After doing the up-and-back drill, your feet should be on A and B. Now jump to C with only your right foot.

2. Using only the right foot, go in order from D to E to C to A to B.

3. Repeat five times.

3. Left Foot

1. You end the right-foot drill on B. Now go to C with your left foot.

2. Using only the left foot, go in order from D to E to C to A to B.

3. Repeat five times.

Figure 11.2 The BFS dot drill performed on a dot drill pad.

4. Both Feet

1. You end the left-foot drill on B. Now go to C with both feet (figure 11.2).

2. With both feet go in order from D to E to C to A to B.

3. Repeat five times.

5. Turn Around

1. You end the both-feet drill on B. Now go to C with both feet.

2. Go to D and E with split feet as in the up-and-back drill (drill 1).

3. Quickly jump and turn 180 degrees to your right and face the other way. You should still be on D and E.

4. Hit C with both feet and then A and B with split feet.

5. Turn quickly again with a 180-degree spin to the left with split feet still on A and B.

6. Repeat five times.

Note that you will be facing the same direction on all the drills except the turn-around drill. A simple phrase to think when doing the right-foot, left-foot, and both-feet drills is "in-out-across":

In to the middle, to C

Out to D

Across to E

In to the middle, to C

Out to A

Across to B

When they first try the dot drill, athletes will find it tiring, and they may appear clumsy. For those reasons athletes should set two goals. The first is to do the drill six times per week, and the second is to improve their time. If they perform the drill six times a week, they will soon be able to do the drills without becoming tired, and they will improve dramatically within a month. To keep motivation high, a coach should time the athletes about twice a month and record their progress and results. Table 11.1 shows the BFS dot drill standards for males and females.

Table 11.1 BFS Dot Drill Standards for Males and Females

Grade	Males	Females
All-American	Under 40 sec	Under 45 sec
Super quick	40-49 sec	45-54 sec
Great	50-59 sec	55-64 sec
Average	60-70 sec	65-75 sec
Needs more work	Over 70 sec	Over 75 sec

BFS dot drill records:

High school boys record: Michael Brown 33.37 sec, Poplar Bluff, Missouri

High school girls record: Kristian Meyers 37.77 sec, Poplar Bluff, Missouri

Jones Brothers—Taking the Triple Crown

Eddie, Daniel, and Aaron believe in a strong work ethic.

Every once in a while you will hear of two brothers winning state championships—but three brothers? Meet the Jones brothers. Winning a state title in wrestling is a significant accomplishment because wrestling is such a competitive sport, especially at the high school level. When two brothers win state titles in the same year, you're talking about an extremely rare occurrence. When three brothers win state championships in the same year, now you're talking about a mathematical phenomenon. But that's exactly what Eddie, Daniel, and Aaron Jones accomplished.

At the 2001 Montana State Wrestling Championships, Eddie, Daniel, and Aaron Jones managed to do what the record books suggest has only been accomplished once before. The brothers wrestled in the 189-, 160-, and 152-pound body weight divisions respectively, which are among the most competitive weight classes, and won. Further, the boys wrestle in the BC school category, which may be considered more competitive than the A and AA divisions. "In this area there are only 12 AA schools, but there are almost four times that many BC schools," says Llew Jones, the boys' father. "The competition in BC is considered harder because of the higher numbers."

Although all the boys felt pressure because the February competition was the last time they would have a chance to accomplish their feat, Aaron, who's 16 and will be a junior this year, had one of the toughest challenges. In the semifinals, the wrestler he was facing was a senior who was ranked number one in the state and had dropped a weight class to face Aaron. Nevertheless, Aaron triumphed over this unexpected obstacle and went on to the finals, sticking his opponent in the first round.

Because wrestling is conducted from lighter to heavier classes, Eddie was the last to wrestle and had a close match with his opponent. "I had beaten him before so it wasn't that I was likely to lose, but I had to go out there and I had to win," says Eddie. "There wasn't really a lot of outside pressure on me to win, but all three of us are competitive and I probably would have gotten crap from my brothers forever if I didn't win."

When asked what it's like to coach these three athletes, Conrad High School head coach Steve Lockyer replied, "It's like a dream come true. Not only do you have kids who are willing to go beyond the extra mile, but you also have the parents who demand, push, and support at home. You can't ask for more than that."

What sets these three brothers apart, according to Coach Lockyer, is a great work ethic. "It started at home a long time ago. Llew has expected big things from them since day one. And with the exception of Aaron, these kids are not great natural athletes—these are just kids who are willing to work and sacrifice to get it done." In fact, the toughest part of coaching them is finding them good workout partners other than each other to challenge them in their training. Llew, who serves as assistant coach, says, "You know, you're only as tough as the person you practice with."

Just how do the Jones boys stack up to the rest of the country? Pretty well. For example, all three brothers were invited to the Denver Nationals, a competition that attracted wrestlers from 40 states in all divisions. In this competition Eddie and Aaron won in their respective classes, and Danny captured third. At the Reno World of Wrestling Championships, Eddie and Daniel took firsts while Aaron finished second. All three brothers have been consistently ranked in the national top 20.

In addition to their wrestling, the Jones brothers have also made their presence felt on the gridiron. When he was 18 Eddie was an all-state linebacker, breaking the school record for tackles, and an all-state fullback. Daniel, who was 17 at the time, made all-conference. Aaron, who was 16, won several awards for his defensive play.

Although they don't compete in Olympic lifting or power lifting, Eddie, Daniel, and Aaron could certainly excel on the lifting platform. Eddie power cleans 275 pounds, squats 380, benches 340, and deadlifts 485. Daniel power cleans 250, squats 360, benches 310, and deadlifts 445. Aaron power cleans 215, squats 330, benches 250, and deadlifts 420. And remember, Daniel and Aaron are relatively light (wrestling at 160 and 152 pounds, respectively) and are performing these lifts without supportive powerlifting gear such as bench shirts and supersuits.

As for academics, Llew makes this the number-one priority with his sons. He has a family policy that if you're not on the honor roll, you don't participate in athletics. Says Coach Lockyer, "I also teach, and it's great to have them in the classroom." Eddie, the oldest, has set the standard for his brothers in this regard by choosing Harvard as his college and selecting pre-med as his major. "I'm only going to wrestle for four more years of my life and maybe a little after that; and for my future, Harvard would take me farther than the big wrestling colleges that were recruiting me." True to form, Daniel and Aaron are also interested in attending Harvard after high school.

Eddie, Daniel, and Aaron are well prepared to take on the challenges ahead. Sure, it's mathematically possible that another set of brothers could match their wrestling success, but I wouldn't count on finding a trio anytime soon who can keep up with the Jones boys.

Five-Phase Plyometric Program

As we coaches become more sophisticated and scientific in our total training programs, we learn that plyometrics can have great value. Athletes who work super hard in the weight room but neglect all other forms of training will not reach their potential. Plyometrics can be the icing on the cake in terms of speed, jumping, and explosiveness.

Frank Costello, in his book *Bounding to the Top,* says, "The athlete stores kinetic energy while descending and converts it to potential energy for the concentric contraction required to respond immediately. The myostatic, or stretch, reflex makes this reaction possible." Former world-class discus thrower Stefan Fernholm states, "Plyometrics played a major role in getting my 40-yard dash down to 4.25 seconds and my vertical jump to 39 inches at a body weight of 270 pounds." Besides the field data of athletic success stories, considerable peer-review research is available to prove that plyometrics work.

For example, in a paper published in the *Journal of Applied Sports Science Research* in 1992, researchers conducted a six-week study on the effects of squatting and plyometrics on the vertical jump. The group that performed just the squat increased their vertical jump 3.3 centimeters (1.3 inches), a significant improvement for six weeks. When plyometrics was combined with squatting, however, the increase was 10.7 centimeters (4.2 inches)! With scientifically documented improvements of that magnitude, you can see why plyometrics is an integral part of the BFS program.

Simply put, plyometric training involves maximum explosive contractions performed as quickly as possible. Your feet should spend as little time as possible in contact with the ground or floor. When you jump up, you use maximum effort. When you bound for height or distance, you go all out. You are teaching your body how to use its strength. You are going to become explosive! Figure 12.1 shows the various heights of BFS readiness boxes. It is important to use a solid box as shown in figure 12.2 rather than the example shown in figure 12.3 in order to prevent injury.

Figure 12.1 Various heights of boxes enable athletes of all levels to perform plyometric exercises.

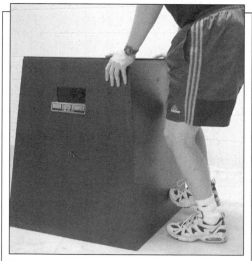

Figure 12.2 With a solid box, the foot safely slides down.

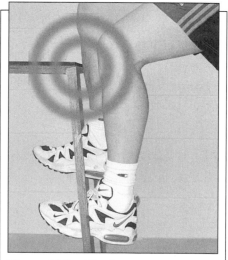

Figure 12.3 The feet can get trapped in an open plyometric box.

JUMPING INTO THE PROGRAM

The BFS plyometric program takes 10 minutes—that's it! Begin by taking 10 quality vertical jumps (VJ). Do the vertical jumps by a wall or basketball standard. Note the height of the first jump and then try to improve with each successive jump. Take a minimum of 15 seconds between vertical jumps. The second phase of our program is to do three sets of three successive standing long jumps. Both the vertical jump and the standing long jump should be tested once a month.

Plyometric box jumping is the third phase (figure 12.4a-d). Assuming that you have the proper boxes, begin by performing five jumps from a 20-inch box and land in a hit position (the position a football player is in when he is about to give or take a hit). Those who have trouble with the 20-inch boxes can use 10-inch boxes (what we call the BFS readiness boxes). Next, jump in the same manner but this time recoil straight up as quickly as possible. On the next series, jump from one box to the floor and then to the next box; repeat five times. Now you are ready to get into it. Follow the same procedure but do it as rapidly as possible. You should have four to five boxes, each about 20 inches high. As you become more advanced, you can raise the height of the last box. For boys, a good jump for the last box is 36 inches, and for girls, 32 inches.

The fourth phase of the program is to jump on a box from a stand. This phase will create interest and enthusiasm for plyometrics. As a coach, you may wish to test a standing box jump once a month.

The final phase can be a series of plyometric bounding drills, which, as the accompanying photos show, are running drills in which the leg drive is exaggerated so that more height and distance are covered with each foot contact (see figure 12.5a-d, page 129).

All these phases may sound like a lot to do in just 10 minutes, but if you are organized, you'll be amazed at the amount of work that you'll accomplish. Divide a class into two main groups; one group can work on speed while the other works on plyometrics. Divide the speed group in half, with one group working technique and the other working sprints. You can also divide the plyometrics group into two groups. Half can be doing bounding, vertical jumps, and standing long jumps while the other half works on box jumping. This training period can be tremendously productive and pay great dividends in improved athletic performance.

STANDING BOX JUMP

One exercise we implement in the BFS program is the standing box jump. Box jumping for height can be a great part of your plyometric

Figure 12.4 Various phases of plyometric box jumping: *(a)* landing on floor, *(b)* vertical jump, *(c)* landing on box, and *(d)* multiple box jumps.

Figure 12.5 Plyometric bounding drills. *(a)* Hurdle jumping, *(b)* side hops, *(c)* bounding for height, and *(d)* bounding for speed.

program and total conditioning program. The concept is similar to going for a max in the weight room and has the same benefit of improved accomplishment.

Box jumping bridges the gap between strength and explosive power. Being able to squat 500 pounds is great, but that alone does not ensure explosive power. Box jumping can help the muscular system contract more quickly and with greater force. Box jumping works through a principle similar to the overload principle in weight training. As the athlete gradually increases the resistance or the weight on the bar, he or she becomes stronger. Likewise, a gradual increase in the height of the plyometric boxes produces an increase in explosive power and jumping ability.

You can measure increases and improvements in jumping ability in several ways. The most common way is to measure an athlete's vertical jump. You can also measure an athlete's standing long jump, either for one jump or for three successive jumps. Another way is to have an athlete jump up onto a box. But the benefits and the mental aspects of the vertical jump are different from those of the standing long jump.

The average high school male athlete with some training should be able to jump up on a 36-inch box, and elite athletes should be able to jump up to 56 inches. When my son Matt was in eighth grade (at five feet, seven and a half inches and 132 pounds), he jumped to a 38-inch height. Reaching that level made him smile for days.

I've seen a lot of great mental adjustment take place as the heights of the boxes were gradually raised. Two tremendous benefits are improved self-concept and greater confidence. You'll hear statements such as, "Wow! I never thought I could do that!" As far as I'm concerned, those benefits alone make box jumping worth the effort.

For the lineman who is six feet, four inches and 270 pounds, benches 450 pounds, squats 600 pounds, vertical jumps 24 inches, and runs only 5.0 seconds, something is missing. Plyometrics can move the VJ to 30 inches and improve the 40-yard dash to a respectable 4.7 seconds. For the running back who runs 4.6 and has average lateral movement, plyometrics can make the difference between being a good player and being a great one. Plyometrics are definitely worth your time!

Speed Training

During the off-season, athletes should perform speed training on Tuesdays and Thursdays and lift on Mondays, Wednesdays, and Fridays. Speed workouts should occur twice per week during the in-season as well.

Athletes should be tested for speed twice per month on either a 40-yard or a 20-yard sprint. They should record their times so that they can chart their progress. Give athletes a trial run at 75 to 90 percent speed and then have them run three timed sprints. They record the best of the three times.

Sprint-training workouts last about 10 minutes. Five of those minutes should be devoted to technique. Concentrate on only one weakness in form at a time—whether it be the position of the head, eyes, back, arms, legs, or foot plant—before going on to another. Video analysis is a great way to learn precisely what needs work. Athletes enjoy seeing themselves, and videotape heightens their awareness of proper sprinting technique.

The remaining five minutes of the speed workout should be devoted to doing 10 all-out quality sprints at distances ranging from 10 to 50 yards. Athletes should have about 30 seconds of rest between sprints so that they are breathing easily before their next sprint. You don't want your athletes' breathing to be labored.

Angela Williams has the best sprint start in the world.

Of course, you must consider that the BFS program is designed for a class setting and for sports that require short-term endurance. For example, football players go all out for 2 to 5 seconds and then must be ready for the next play within 10 to 30 seconds. Athletes training for maximum speed need more rest time between sets (one popular method is to rest one minute for every 10 yards of running).

When the weather is bad, do not stop sprinting. Let your competition take it easy. In Minnesota, waiting for warm weather would mean avoiding sprints for six months. Replace 40-yard sprints outdoors with 20-yard sprints indoors. Times for the two distances will generally differ by about two seconds. Thus a 3.0 seconds for 20 yards is equivalent to a 5.0 seconds for 40 yards.

TEN WAYS TO IMPROVE SPEED

Carl Lewis ran 9.92 at the Seoul Olympics for a new American record in the 100 meters. Lewis won the gold medal after Ben Johnson tested positive for steroids. Lewis stated that he had run as fast as he could. Not true—Lewis made four critical errors and probably could have run as fast as 9.87 seconds that day. First, he turned his head three times to look at Johnson—that's three errors. By turning his head, Lewis was unable to be as fluid as he could have been. His fourth error was letting up two or three yards before the finish line.

Here are 10 guaranteed ways to improve your speed:

1. Sprint train twice per week, minimum.
2. Do 10 sprints, varying from 10 to 50 yards.
3. Time your sprints twice per month (record and chart all times).
4. Sprint all year round. In bad weather, run the 20-yard dash for time.
5. Use video analysis. It can be extremely valuable!
6. Do flexibility training six times per week. To improve speed, you must do it correctly.
7. Do plyometrics twice per week, minimum.
8. Parallel squat. If you squat but don't go parallel, you will not improve speed maximally. You must do parallel squats to parallel, period!
9. To build and stretch the glutes and hamstrings at the same time, perform the straight-leg deadlift, a lift critical to speed improvement.
10. Do power cleans to develop an explosive start.

FAST FROM THE START

One of the most important aspects of running fast is getting a good start. Here are the proven ways to get the best start possible, as demonstrated by Kevin Devine, fastest player in the NFL in 1998-99. Kevin, who was with the Jacksonville Jaguars, used the modified BFS track stance at the NFL combine and ran the 40 in 4.2 seconds.

Learn the modified BFS track stance. I guarantee that no college scout or pro scout makes a note about whether you use a track stance or a football stance. All they do is mark down your time, so you might as well do it right.

- **Hands.** Your thumb and first finger should be on the starting line. Your fingertips should support your weight.
- **Feet.** A rule of thumb is to place one foot 4 to 6 inches behind the line and the other foot back an additional 12 inches.
- **Head.** Keep your head down. When it is up, you will tighten up.

Figure 13.1 shows a poor starting position. The hips are high, the back is arched, and the sprinter is looking at the ground. He will be unable to get full power from his legs and will have to take time to adjust his posture and focus to get started—time a sprinter cannot afford to lose.

Now look at figure 13.2. The back knee is down, and the body is relaxed. You are "on your mark." Raise your hips higher than your shoulders. Shift your weight as far forward as possible. Your shoulders should be way out in front of your hands. Although this position is uncomfortable, you'll have great forward momentum for a super start. You are now at "get set." One arm comes way up on "set." On "Go!" that arm punches forward with great power and the back leg simultaneously does the same. The left arm and right leg explode forward at the same time.

As you begin to sprint, you stay low and extend your back leg completely. Keep your arms at a right angle and your arm movement extremely vigorous.

Figure 13.1 Example of poor starting position (hips are too high.)

BFS SPRINT TECHNIQUE SYSTEM

Sprinting can be very technical, which is one reason why many sprinters don't hit their peak until they are in their late 20s or even their 30s. But you can master the basics if you follow the BFS sprint technique system. This system consists of eight techniques (see figure 13.3):

1. Your head should be upright

2. Your eyes should be fixed, looking straight ahead (on target).

Figure 13.2 Better starting position, although head is slightly higher than optimal.

3. Your toes should point straight ahead.

4. Your back should be upright and slightly arched.

5. Your shoulders should rotate vigorously, with the elbows fixed at 90-degree angles.

6. Your wrists should simulate a whip action as the shoulders rotate back.

7. Your feet should make the initial plant directly under the hips, not out in front of the body.

8. Your forward leg should initially lift forward, not up. The lower leg should hang before planting with the foot and toes up. Your back knee should extend fully on the follow-through, or end-of-the-leg drive.

Those are the basics of BFS speed training. If you follow those simple guidelines and train consistently, you'll be amazed at how fast you can become.

Figure 13.3 Kevin Devine, formerly the fastest man in the NFL, demonstrates the perfect form for the sprint start.

BFS 1-2-3-4 Flexibility Program

There are two reasons why the BFS 1-2-3-4 flexibility program are important to any athlete's training. First, we stretch for speed and jumping power (Athletes often shave two-tenths of a second off their time and increases their vertical jump by four inches.) Second, we do each stretch perfect, using the principles of the 6 absolutes.

We've found, after giving thousands of BFS clinics over the past quarter of a century, that stretching is the one component most often missing in an athlete's training. This omission is odd considering the tremendous amount of research available on the value of stretching, not just for athletes but also for nonathletes who simply want to improve their quality of life. Our society is increasingly overweight, and in becoming a nation of couch potatoes we have made ourselves far less flexible than ever before. BFS is determined to reverse that trend.

The only way to make that happen for our athletes is to incorporate flexibility training into a total program. BFS regards stretching as a separate exercise regimen, like plyometrics and weightlifting. Stretching is not part of a warm-up or cool-down for physical activity that athletes need to do only occasionally. They must stretch daily, in both the off-season and the in-season. A stretching regimen involves serious work, concentration, and adherence to proper technique.

Just as a coach analyzes every aspect of an athlete's performance, we take stretching seriously and look at every detail. Everything must be perfect. We want our athletes to look like sprinters when stretching, so every limb and every joint is straight and perfect. We use the six absolutes and ask, "Are the knees aligned; are the toes aligned?" Most coaches don't consider those important aspects of stretching. Attention to detail is what makes our program unique and, more important, what makes our program work.

The BFS 1-2-3-4 flexibility program is perfect for everyone, although some individuals may progress faster than others do and achieve different results. In addition, women tend to be more flexible than men are, especially on the adductor (inner-thigh) stretch. Athletes should avoid comparing themselves to others and just focus on self-improvement by making themselves more flexible.

Regarding individual differences, for every athlete who is super tight, another may have too much flexibility. In wrestling, I've seen kids who are so incredibly flexible that you just can't pin them, no matter how hard you try, because their extreme flexibility allows them to wriggle out of a pin. But they never win because they're so weak. That's the reason we sometimes hear athletes say, "Why do I need to be really flexible? There's Joe, and he's really flexible and he can't jump 10 inches! So what's the big deal about flexibility?" The goal is balance. The idea is not to be one-sided and set out to become super flexible, but to have balance. Our aim is to make strong athletes more flexible and flexible athletes stronger. When athletes have both assets going for them—flexibility and strength—they really have an edge.

Athletes can gain several specific benefits by following the BFS 1-2-3-4 flexibility program:

- Increased joint range of motion
- Increased speed
- Improved overall performance
- Improved posture
- Decreased number and severity of injuries

The benefits of stretching go beyond injury prevention and rehabilitation. Many movements in athletics require exceptional levels of flexibility that may take years of stretching to develop and daily workouts to maintain. For example, if baseball pitchers can get their arms back a little farther, they will throw harder and faster. When golfers can get their arms and shoulders back two inches farther, they can add 20 yards to their drives. As an example, my son Mark, who is not particularly strong, has such a huge range-of-motion arch in his golf swing that he can hit the ball 300 yards! And if a football player can improve flexibility in the hip-flexor area so that his stride length is two inches greater, that alone may improve a 40-yard-dash time by two 10ths of a second.

The BFS 1-2-3-4 flexibility program is especially useful for increasing running speed. Kevin Devine, one of the fastest players in professional football, believes that stretching is key to developing speed. Says Devine, "If you don't stretch hard every day, you will never be as fast as you could be." Although he certainly has a genetic gift for running, Devine says he has made the most of his talents with stretching. "You stretch to win," he says. "It's that simple."

BFS STRETCHING PROGRAM

Our mission at BFS is to provide coaches with a stretching program that will benefit athletes and be feasible in coaching situations where time, facilities, and number of athletes are considerations. We considered all these factors in developing our recommendations for the most appropriate stretching regimen for BFS. We decided that the simplest yet most practical and effective program would be exercises that use the static-stretch method.

With static stretching, muscles are passively lengthened and then held in the stretched position for prolonged periods. The advantage of static stretches is that athletes can learn them easily and perform them without a partner. Done correctly, static stretching produces less muscle tension and offers more safety than other stretching methods do. Injuries from static stretching are virtually nonexistent, a claim that cannot be made about other stretching methods.

Although static stretching can be one of the safest types of exercise, athletes should not stretch under certain conditions. For example, stretching the muscles around a recently fractured bone or around an area that has been recently sprained or strained, especially around the back or neck, is usually not a good idea. Here are a few other guidelines:

1. **Warm up.** Stretching is not a warm-up. To avoid injury, you want your muscles to be warm before you stretch. The BFS dot drill is a perfect warm-up because it will help you break a light sweat.

2. **Stretch in the proper environment.** A firm, nonskid mat is ideal for stretching, and the area you're stretching in should be free of distractions, if possible, so that you can concentrate.

3. **Stretch slowly and gently.** Be forceful when you stretch. Always stretch slowly, moving gradually into each stretch and easing out of every stretch smoothly and slowly.

4. Listen to your pain. Do not force a joint to the point that you feel pain. You do need to be uncomfortable but do not extend a joint beyond the point of discomfort. Never yank, pull, or jerk but do stretch hard. You should be sweating at the end of a stretching workout.

5. Concentrate on breathing. Proper breathing methods can significantly enhance the quality of your stretching program. Don't hold your breath. You should breathe normally, trying to ease deeper into a stretch during each exhale.

6. Don't overdo it. Although this issue is subject to continual debate, you'll gain the greatest benefit from stretching by holding each position for at least 30 seconds. But for beginners, especially those who are extremely tight, performing three sets of 10-second holds is an effective alternative.

7. Personalize your routine. You should consider your individual needs when designing a stretching program. For example, if you are hypermobile in the knee joint, striving to increase the flexibility of your hamstrings may not be a good idea. If you are an athlete in a sport that requires exceptional flexibility in one area of the body, such as a swimmer who needs flexible shoulders, you may want to add a few additional stretches for that area.

8. Vary your routine. You should occasionally vary the stretches you perform. In this chapter we'll provide you with several alternative stretches, as well as a list of stretches you should avoid because they may cause more harm than good. We recommend that you experiment with these other stretches only after you have performed our standard BFS 1-2-3-4 flexibility program for several months.

9. Stretch after workouts. Most coaches and sport therapists agree that the best time to stretch is after a workout, especially when it comes to preventing hamstring pulls. Dr. Michael Ripley, a specialist in flexibility therapy, has worked with 10 sprinters who won medals in the Sydney Olympics, several of whom he treated for hamstring problems before the Olympics. Ripley says that after training, muscles often develop a higher level of tension than they had before the training. "This tension will cause muscles to shorten, and without poststretching I've found that over time this causes shortening of the athlete's range of motion. In my opinion it's most important to stretch immediately after the workout because you help keep the body symmetrical. In contrast, if you waited several hours, you'd have to stretch for a considerably longer time to achieve the same effects."

If the training environment is crowded and time is short, such as in a classroom situation, athletes would be better off stretching at home. If facilities are spacious and plenty of time is available, the ideal scenario would be to stretch after performing the dot drill and again at the end of the workout.

The System

We have created a stretching program that takes about 10 minutes per session and thoroughly stretches every major area of the body, especially the trunk, hips, and legs. The program has been field tested in thousands of high schools and used by countless athletes of all ages, so we know it works. After athletes learn the program, they can stretch anytime, anywhere, without a partner.

The BFS stretching program is as easy as 1-2-3-4. I say that because those numbers help everyone understand and remember the program. Specifically, the program consists of 11 stretches, divided into four groups, performed in the following order:

1. On a bench   3. On a wall

2. Standing   4. On the floor

The numbers 1-2-3-4 refer both to the order in which the athlete performs each group of exercises and to the approximate amount of time, in minutes, the athlete devotes to each group of exercises. Thus, the athlete spends one minute performing stretches while sitting on a bench, two minutes while standing, three minutes in contact with a wall, and at least four minutes (performing five stretches) while sitting on the floor.

Each stretch should be held for at least 30 seconds, although it's fine to hold a stretch up to 60 seconds to create a higher degree of relaxation. Stretches involving single limbs are performed for 30 seconds on each side, for a total of one minute. Beginners have the option of holding each stretch for only 10 seconds, performing three sets per stretch to equal 30 seconds. Now let's get on to the workout (figure 14.1, page 143).

One on the Bench (One Stretch, About One Minute)

Perform the hamstring stretch. Keep your leg locked out and the toes vertical or back toward the chest. Pull your upper body forward, looking straight ahead and spreading the chest. Perform for both legs.

Two in the Air (Two Stretches, About Two Minutes)

Perform the both the latissimus stretch and the pectoral stretch. For the latissimus stretch, cross your hands and raise your arms above your head and as far back as possible. On the pectoral stretch, cross your hands behind your back and raise your arms up and back as far as possible. Do not lean over.

Three on the Wall (Three Stretches, About Three Minutes)

Perform the following three stretches for three minutes on the wall.

■ **Backleg stretch.** Keeping your feet flat on the ground, one foot ahead of the other, and your hands on the wall, move your hips forward. Your back foot and toes should be straight, pointed forward. Perform for both legs.

■ **Achilles stretch.** This stretch is like the backleg stretch except that you keep your knee slightly bent, with your heel one inch off the floor. Squat down to increase the intensity of the stretch. Perform for both legs.

■ **Quadriceps stretch.** With one hand on the wall, grasp one foot and pull your leg straight up and away from your buttocks. Hold your knee at a 90-degree angle. You should pull the knee straight back, never out to the side. Perform for both legs.

Four on the Floor (Five Stretches, About Four or Five Minutes)

Perform the following five stretches over a four- to five-minute period.

■ **Abdominal stretch.** Lie flat on the floor. Put your hands on the floor, shoulder-width apart (as if you were about to perform a push-up), and extend your elbows to create an arch in your back.

■ **Adductor stretch.** With your feet as far apart as possible, grab your ankles or feet and pull your torso slowly toward the floor. If you can't reach your toes, place your fists on the floor behind you and push forward.

■ **Gluteus maximus stretch.** Begin twisting your torso carefully and then press one knee firmly with the opposite arm, forcing your knee to the other side of the lower leg. Switch to the other side.

■ **Groin stretch.** Sit with the bottoms of your feet together and grab your ankles. Pull in and press down toward the floor with your elbows on your thighs.

■ **Hip-flexor stretch.** Place one foot 24 inches in front of your opposite knee. Now place your hands on your bent knee and force your hips forward and down. Spread your chest and keep your eyes straight ahead and your back upright. Do not bend over or put your elbows on your knee—you will be wasting your time. Perform for both legs.

Hamstring

Lat and pec

Backleg stretch

Achilles

Quads

Abs

Adductor

Glute

Groin

Hip flexor

Figure 14.1 Various stretch routines.

Measuring Progress

As in weight training, measuring progress and setting records in the stretching program will help keep an athlete's motivation high. To measure progress with the BFS 1-2-3-4 flexibility program, we recommend that athletes take the sit-and-reach test at least once a month. The sit-and-reach test measures flexibility in the back of the legs and in the lower back. To perform the test, you sit on the floor with your legs together (putting your legs against a board or a partner's hand will help keep you from moving). Reach as far as possible and hold for three seconds. Place a yardstick with the six-inch mark at your heels and the one-inch mark closest to your body. Reach as far as possible and check results (see figure 14.2). Table 14.1 lists the BFS standards for the sit-and-reach test.

After a few weeks of BFS stretching exercises, you will begin to enjoy significant improvements in flexibility and overall athletic ability. Just 11 minutes of intelligent stretching each day is a painless way to move closer to your goals. Athletic programs at many schools (maybe even your competition's) neglect flexibility training. So it's a smart move to use the BFS 1-2-3-4 flexibility program to put those critical minutes to work for you.

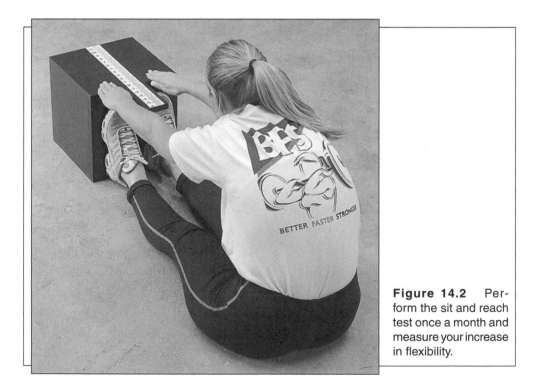

Figure 14.2 Perform the sit and reach test once a month and measure your increase in flexibility.

Table 14.1   BFS Standards for Sit-and-Reach Test

Grade	Males	Females
Excellent	6 in. past heels	8 in. past heels
Good	2 in. past heels	4 in. past heels
Fair	2 in. short of heels	0 in. at heels
Poor	6 in. short of heels	4 in. short of heels

PART IV

Program Administration

Organization, Weight-Room Design, and Safety

Thousands of coaches across America use the Bigger Faster Stronger program or are in the process of implementing it. The following questions are often asked of our certified coaches, either at clinics or through our toll-free lines:

- How do I get the BFS program working at my school?
- How do I organize my training periods?
- How should I set up my weight room to run the program?
- What equipment do I need to run the program?

We at BFS believe that you should build your program around six core exercises: the box squat, parallel squat, hex-bar deadlift, power clean, towel bench, and bench press. Make certain that your program setup, organization, and equipment allow all your athletes to complete the six core lifts in one week. After you have accomplished that goal, you can begin to look for auxiliary equipment based on the amount of time, space, and money you have in the program. Always build your core stations first.

WEIGHT-ROOM DESIGN

One of the strengths of the BFS program is its adaptability to almost any situation. BFS certified coaching staff members suggested the following weight-room designs for two high schools. Figure 15.1 shows a weight room built from scratch that can handle 48 athletes using our system, and figure 15.2 shows a weight room that already had some equipment and has been modified to fit the BFS program.

Figure 15.1 A weight room should be large enough to allow many athletes to safely train at the same time.

Figure 15.2
Poor weight room design will slow the progress of your athletes and your program.

Table 15.1 lists equipment suggestions for each of the four core lift stations.

Do-It-All Stations

The hottest new trend in weight-room equipment and organization is to have one station do it all for core lifts and some major auxiliaries. The Ohio University strength and conditioning facility exemplifies this trend. With 10,000 square feet and 33 individual do-it-all stations, the Bobcat training facility is one of the most impressive weight rooms among Division I universities. Athletes can do benches, inclines, squats, presses, jerks, cleans, and various other lifts at each station. In addition, each station has a chin-up bar and a pair of ab slings. Only bumper plates are used, and the 33 stations include a whopping 17,800 pounds of plates. By having three athletes per station, a strength coach can train 99 athletes at the same time on the same core lift.

Table 15.1 Equipment for Four Core Stations

Power clean	Squat and box-squat	Hex-bar deadlift	Bench and towel-bench station
• Lifting platform (or two rubber mats) • 310 lb Olympic set • Set of bumper plates (5, 10, 25, 45 lb) • 15 lb Olympic bar • Two bumper plate racks (one on each side of platform) • Chalk bin • Wrist straps • Two lifting belts (small, medium)	• Squat rack or power rack • 500 lb Olympic set • Three squat boxes (small, medium, large) • Two plate racks (one on each side of rack) • Two lifting belts (small, medium)	• Lifting platform (or two rubber mats) • Hex bar (with the option of a mega-hex bar) • Two plate racks (one on each side of platform) • Two 45 lb bumper plates • 400 lb total in plate weights • Wrist straps • Three lifting belts (small, medium, large)	• Olympic bench • 310 lb Olympic set • Towel-bench pad

What are the advantages of these stations? Each core lift has a unique time constraint. For example, it takes longer to complete a given number of sets on the parallel squat than it does on the bench press. Therefore, if you have four squat stations and four bench stations with a system of rotating from one to another, you can run into problems. The athletes doing the bench finish their sets before the athletes who are squatting. What do you do? Well, the athletes could stretch, do a burnout set, or do an auxiliary lift. So the situation need not be unproductive or a waste of time. The one-station, do-it-all concept, however, is more efficient. Coaching is easier because everyone is doing the same lift. Your time management is more precise and controlled. The athletes can be more intense and competitive with everyone doing the same lift. Finally, in most cases, the one-station approach can save space. Figures 15.3 and 15.4 demonstrate the BFS Elite all-in-one training systems for the bench and power clean.

Figure 15.3   Bench station.

Figure 15.4   Power-clean station.

Just Like Practice

A great way to organize a high school or college weight-training program is to handle it just like a football practice or a practice for another team sport. Let your competition's coach prescribe a workout and then sit at a desk reading a newspaper. Here are some better ideas:

■ **Require the same discipline.** Athletes should be on time and have the feeling that they are participating in a sport practice in the weight room. Athletes should be attentive, hustling, and team oriented. Let your competition allow their weight training session to be a social hour.

■ **Instill a team-concept approach.** Make gains as a team. Take team pride in individual records. You could have contests between juniors and seniors or between your team and another team. As a coach you must be active, just as you are in a team practice, constantly motivating and teaching. Let your competition make workouts dull and lacking team pride.

■ **Organize time and total program efficiently.** Wouldn't it be great if the opposing football coach spent all his practice time on offense and did absolutely nothing with defense or the kicking game? Let your competition work only on weights or concentrate largely on the upper body or bodybuilding. With the BFS total program, you work each important area with just the right amount of time. You work on flexibility and agility every day. You lift three times per week, concentrating on the legs and hips with total-body lifting movements such as the squat and the power clean. You work on speed and plyometric training twice per week in the off-season. You also spend time working on technique skills by position and sport. Setting aside some time (five minutes) on Tuesdays and Thursdays to discuss subjects such as nutrition, rest, and strategy is appropriate. You could also offer a short motivational story once a week.

■ **Do some activities outside class!** Does a forward in hockey go on the ice and practice with the goalie? Does a quarterback go out and throw with his receivers on their own? Of course! Why not extend this concept to your training program? Let your competition stretch for 15 minutes of the 42-minute physical education class period. Let your competition become frustrated and exclaim: "We can't get to it. There isn't enough time!"

Give your athletes a chance to excel, a chance to reach their potential. If your team is truly committed to winning, most of them will stretch and do agility drills outside class time. All a coach has to do is test on Tuesdays and Thursdays to verify the athletes' commitment. Athletes can also do some plyometric, speed, and technique work on their own.

Having your athletes sign commitment contracts or goal cards can help make success happen.

■ **Require disciplined spotting and good technique.** A gymnastics coach wouldn't say, "OK, this group is the B squad. Do anything you want." Your competition might be that way in the weight room, but you should always have spotters who encourage their teammates to give their best. Every athlete should be keenly aware of the coaching techniques of every lift and accept the responsibility of being a coach while spotting.

■ **Modify the program intelligently.** One of the workouts in our four-week cycle is to do five sets of five, and another is a 5-4-3-2-1 workout. A 42-minute physical education period isn't long enough to do that many sets. Therefore, we recommend doing three sets of five and 5-3-1 for those respective workouts. This modification sacrifices only a small amount of physical development and allows enough time to do it right. Be creative in your use of time and equipment.

■ **Don't scrimmage.** All coaches should do some lifting, but there are too many disadvantages to coaches doing their own training during the athletes' workout time. Although athletes respect a coach who keeps in shape, it is just too difficult to teach and motivate properly if you're busy lifting. Occasionally, a coach with the required ability might demonstrate things like intensity, poundage, and technique.

WEIGHT-ROOM ESSENTIALS

Several items are necessary in every weight room. At BFS we recommend having lifting belts, knee wraps, wrist straps, and lifting chains available.

Lifting Belts

Lifting belts give physiological and psychological support. Coaches should have three kinds of belts—the power-lifting belt, the Olympic lifting belt, and the training belt—in a weight room.

■ **Power-lifting belt.** The power-lifting belt, also known as a power belt or a squat belt, is a double-notched four-inch belt used in the sport of power lifting. This belt is the same width all the way around (see figure 15.5). Many power belts on the market are twice the thickness of a noncompetitive leather belt. Athletes should use this belt when they squat because it provides frontal support in keeping the body upright and sitting tall. Athletes should use a power belt in competition and for setting new personal bests.

■ **Lifting belt.** This belt is about the same size as the power belt but tapers around the front of the body in the buckle area. It may not be as thick or as heavy as the power belt (the official size of the Olympic lifting belt for competition is 10 centimeters, which is slightly smaller than four inches). See figure 15.6. This belt is most effective for training and competing in the Olympic lifts, the snatch, and the clean and jerk. The Olympic lifting belt enables the lifter to bend down without having the belt dig into the stomach, and it provides sufficient support during the action of the lifts. This belt can also be used effectively in the deadlift because the taper in the front allows for a full bend-over. Throwers can use this belt for the hammer, discus, and shot because of its support and allowance of flexibility to the athlete.

Figure 15.5   Power-lifting belt.

■ **Training belt.** Athletes, lifters, and hobbyists often use a six-inch noncompetitive belt, which is six inches wide in the back and tapers down to two inches in the front. Many feel that the six-inch belt gives the best support for the lower back (figure 15.7). Sanctioned power lifting or Olympic lifting meets don't allow use of this belt, which is for personal training only. If an athlete really likes the feel of it, it's an excellent way to train.

Figure 15.6   Lifting belt.

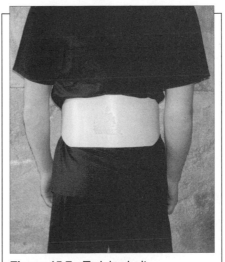

Figure 15.7   Training belt.

Knee Wraps

Knee wraps should be available to all athletes but should be used sparingly. Some lifters wrap their knees for every set. This, I believe, is wrong. Squatting with knee wraps hinders the development of the tendons and ligaments of the knee.

But nearly all power lifters wear knee wraps in competition. A lifter can squat more weight with knee wraps. Therefore, when athletes are going for heavy sets or new one-rep maxes, knee wraps give beneficial physiological and psychological support. Some athletes will have sore or tender knees. Knee wraps often make squatting easier and more tolerable. Knee wraps also keep the knee joint warm and therefore better lubricated with synovial fluid.

Wrist Straps

Wrist straps can also be used in the power clean, the hex-bar deadlift, or any heavy type of pulling exercises. These exercises are not designed to develop wrist and hand strength. Therefore, it would be a mistake to allow weakness in the hand and wrist to deter or hamper total-body development in these power exercises. The wrist straps help an athlete focus on the acceleration of the bar and prevent slippage and skin abrasions to the palm area. To develop grabbing power, however, some athletes playing certain positions in football might not want to use straps.

Wrist straps should be one and one-half inches wide and long enough to wrap once completely around the bar. Straps made from slick materials are not recommended. Good straps are made from canvas or leather. All straps eventually wear out, so it is important to check frequently for tears that may lead to breakage. Athletes must not lift with worn straps.

Using wrist straps is relatively easy, but you must develop some finger dexterity and coordination to use them quickly and efficiently. At first, using straps may seem awkward, but with practice you will quickly get the hang of it. To begin, simply put your hand through the loop. The end of the strap should be on the same side of the bar as the thumb. Then you are ready to wrap the strap around the bar as tightly as possible. Now grip the rolled-up strap with your fingers and thumb to lock the strap into place. Follow the same procedure with the other hand.

Wrist Wraps

Many athletes get sore wrists from doing power cleans or even bench presses. Incorrect technique or poor flexibility often causes this soreness. The power clean, when done correctly, will rest on the deltoids as the athlete racks the bar. The wrists should never fully or primarily support the bar.

I recommend wrist wraps as a training aid for the clean. They give great support to the wrist and might prevent a wrist injury if an athlete has incorrect technique. I always wear them while doing cleans. They feel good and probably give some psychological support. Once you try them you won't want to lift without them.

I also recommend doing a simple wrist flexibility exercise before doing a power clean. This exercise takes only 15 seconds with each wrist. Pull back on the fingers as shown until the backs of the fingers touch the top of the deltoids. Bring the elbow straight out in front as in the finished rack position of the clean.

Lifting Chains

Lifting chains can be used as squat and bench-press variations. Variation is the key to success in breaking records and not becoming stuck on those dreaded plateaus. Therefore, instead of towel benches, athletes can do chain benches. Instead of box squats or front squats, they can do chain squats. The lifting chains can also be used for auxiliary lifts such as the incline press.

I suggest that you provide your athletes with three different chains: a varsity chain that adds about 25 pounds to a squat and 15 pounds to a bench press, an all-state chain that adds about 40 pounds to a squat and 25 pounds to a bench press, and an all-American chain that adds about 55 pounds to a squat and 37 pounds to a bench press.

Normally, adding about 10 percent at the easiest point is most beneficial, which is the reason for using different sized chains. For example, I would not want to put on 37 extra pounds for an athlete who only bench presses 150 pounds. That much weight would not work as intended. I would not want to add 55 pounds for an athlete who parallel squats 215 pounds. That much weight would prove too difficult. But for someone who parallel squats or box squats 500 or more pounds, the 55-pound all-American chain would be a substantial but still realistic challenge that would produce the intended results. Here are some simple guidelines about which chain to use:

- Use the varsity chain for athletes who bench less than 200 pounds and squat less than 300 pounds.
- Use the all-state chain for athletes who bench between 200 and 300 pounds, and squat between 300 and 400 pounds.
- Use the all-American chain for athletes who bench over 300 pounds and squat over 400 pounds.

Keep in mind that two chains will fit easily on each side of the bar, allowing you to create different combinations. By putting the all-state and all-American chains on together, you can add 62 pounds on the bench and 95 pounds on the squat.

For recording purposes, I recommend recording what is on the bar plus the code of whatever chain you are using. Use "VC" for the varsity chain, "AS" for the all-state chain, and "AA" for the all-American chain. For example, an athlete who does 185 pounds plus the varsity chain would record.

Lifting chains are useful at all levels, from junior high athletes to the most advanced athletes. By having chains of three different weights, you can use different combinations to create even more challenges and variations. It's hard not to be pumped up about all the possibilities and the potential edge you can gain.

SAFETY AND LIABILITY GUIDELINES

Coaches and fitness instructors have a responsibility to present the benefits of weight training. They also have a duty to warn individuals about the potential dangers associated with participation. Strategically placed and well-designed signs are an inexpensive, simple, and often overlooked strategy to inform and warn weight-room users. Signs may not ensure a participant's safety, but they can lower the chance of injury. Well-planned signs help us meet our duty to warn and inform while decreasing the chance of injury. They also demonstrate our concern and credibility.

Remember, the BFS program works to condition all athletes in a coordinated, complete training system across the board, no matter what the sport. To accomplish that goal, all coaches should be unified on the BFS program and philosophy and each should contribute and give support to the supervision, maintenance, and financing of the weight-room facility. From that point, each coach is free to choose auxiliary exercises or methods to augment his or her particular sport.

Washington County High–Smashing Records

Greg Shepard (far right) with athletes and coaches at Washington County High School.

BFS clinician Coach Rick Tomberlin has it going on at Washington County High School in Sandersville, Georgia. In his seven years with the Golden Hawks, Tomberlin has amassed an 85-11 record, including three state championships.

Coach Tomberlin and his team made it a goal to take the BFS dead lift national record of 730 pounds to a new level. For the Golden Hawks, this meant 51 players needed to lift 500 pounds and 11 players needed to get to the 600-pound level. This can be a tricky technique for both lifter and spotter, but Coach Tomberlin and his athletes make it look easy. At a BFS clinic they demonstrated how they met their goal.

Athletes began with a 20-minute warm-up, including agilities, stretching, form running, and sprinting. Next they split into three groups with one group doing three sets of five on the parallel squat. The other two groups did the same sets and reps on the bench and the power clean. Many teams would have been exhausted after this routine, but not the Golden Hawks! This was just their warm-up!

Coach Tomberlin then roped off two platforms, each with 500 pounds on the bar. Then player after player dead-lifted 500 pounds. All 51 players hit the goal. Then 600 pounds was loaded onto the bar. Eleven players were able to do it! The audience was wild with excitement but the show wasn't over yet.

Tyler Biggins, a 290-pound starter stepped forward. A new record weight was eased onto the bar—seven 45's on each end along with a 25 and 5 pound plate. Tyler chalked up and after tightening the lift straps around the bar, pulled with all his might as the bar inched upward. He did it!

Coach Tomberlin and his athletes attribute their success to team loyalty, confidence, self-esteem, attitude, togetherness, and the success of the BFS program to bring them to new heights on and off the football field!

BFS Nutrition Plan

Each of us is responsible for our own greatness, and we must eat well to perform our best. I want to point you in the right direction when it comes to proper nutrition, because in my many years of coaching I have come to realize firsthand that most high school athletes don't eat well.

This is not a nutrition book. My goal is to help those who might rate an F in nutrition improve to a C, or maybe improve from a D to a B. One way to do that is simply to avoid what I call the five lethal foods. Making that one change can make a big improvement in overall health and, consequently, in athletic performance. But it doesn't have to stop there. At the end of this chapter are some resources to help you score an A in nutrition, and it's up to you to decide how much you want to improve. Keeping this advice in mind, let's find out why so many athletes eat poorly and what can be done about it.

Some of the reasons that athletes don't eat well may be that more mothers work outside the home, more households have only one parent, more young people eat at fast-food places and quick marts, and more advertising tempts us to eat poorly. Many young athletes have to prepare meals by themselves. Parents may give their children money to eat out on their own instead of preparing healthy meals for them. Fast-food chains commonly offer special deals on meals consisting of a hamburger, fries, and a soft drink. Convenience stores entice kids with video games and the junkiest of junk food. All this points to a need for more emphasis on eating right, especially for athletes.

BFS NUTRITIONAL RATING CHART

The BFS nutrition plan has been in effect for many years with excellent results. We rate our meals on a scale of 0 to 10. Any good food from one of the basic food groups receives 2 points. Examples include dairy products like milk, cheese, and eggs; meat products such as beef, poultry, and fish; bread and cereal group items; and fruits and vegetables. Each food is worth 2 points. A huge amount of any one item receives a single bonus point (five eggs would receive a total of 3 points). Junk foods such as french fries receive no points. The maximum points for any one meal or snack is 10. A salad or sandwich that has everything gets a maximum of 5 points. Water with a meal is 2 points. Pop, candy, donuts, pastries, coffee, tea, or alcoholic beverages get 0 points. Table 16.1 shows how the diets of three athletes would rate.

The national average is 17 points. If an athlete does not get at least 25 points per day, we recommend that he or she take a food supplement and a multiple vitamin. In our example, athletes John and Mary both have nutritionally sound diets (and note that Mary's diet is nonfattening). Bill raised his hand during a clinic and said that he wanted to get bigger, faster, and stronger. Yet he didn't realize how bad his diet was until we took a close look at it. Bill said he didn't have time to fix breakfast, the school lunch was no good, and his mom left a pizza in the freezer and cookies for a snack. If Bill would fix himself cereal, milk, toast, and juice for breakfast; eat the school lunch; drink milk for dinner and eat some fruit; and have milk, juice, and a banana for snacks in addition to what he already ate, he would push his point total to the 30-point level. The beauty of this system is that Bill wouldn't have to do any cooking. He just has to follow the plan and add up his points.

This nutritional rating system is simple for kids to understand. Breakfast, lunch, dinner, and snacks are each rated according to a point system. A maximum of 40 points may be earned daily. Here is the BFS nutritional rating chart that breaks down the daily point total:

30-40 points: great

25-29 points: good

20-24 points: fair

15-19 points: poor

10-14 points: very poor

5-9 points: drastic

0-4 points: death!

Table 16.1 BFS Nutrition Plan

	John	Points	Mary	Points	Bill	Points
Breakfast	• 2 eggs • juice • 2 milks • bacon • toast	10	• grape-fruit • toast • poached egg • skim milk	8	none	0
Lunch	• 2 big sand-wiches • 3 milks • apple • cookies	10	• yogurt • water • celery • apple	8	• cola • French fries	0
Dinner	• roast beef • peas • salad • milk • orange	10	• salad • skim milk • orange	9	• pizza • cola	3
Snacks	• milk • bananas • ice cream	6	• apple • water • carrots	6	• cookies • cola	0
Totals		36		31		3

SETTING NUTRITIONAL GOALS

The second part of the BFS nutrition plan is providing the motivation of setting and meeting goals. At a BFS clinic the first goal we set on our way to becoming champions is committing ourselves to getting 30 nutritional points every day. Coaches put "30 (5)" on their goal cards, meaning that each of them commits to asking five different kids daily how they're doing on their 30 points. In 30 days the players should have formed good eating habits, which should pay big dividends, not only physically but academically as well.

Gaining Weight

Each of the two basic ways of gaining weight depends on the consumption of calories exceeding the expenditure of calories. Many athletes expend 5,000 or more calories daily. Therefore, they must eat a huge amount to gain weight. The first way to gain weight is to eat a big 30 points, never miss a workout, especially squats, and have a big snack after dinner. The snack should be something like two big meat-and-cheese sandwiches and four glasses of milk.

The second way to gain weight is to take a weight-gain protein supplement, the best being whey protein. All food supplements should be mixed in a blender, with bananas, fruit, ice cream, and so forth added for extra flavor and calories. The athlete should weigh and record the number every day. If the athlete doesn't gain weight after two or three days, he or she must consume more calories. As long as the person follows the total BFS nutritional plan, weight gains will be from desirable lean muscle mass.

The Real Truth About Fat

We are eating much less fat than we did 20 years ago, but the incidence of obesity has jumped 30 percent in the last decade. The occurrence of type 2 diabetes has tripled in the same period. Strokes and coronary heart disease are also occurring more frequently. Fat is not the problem, but most people think it is. We have replaced fat with carbohydrates, which is really starch and sugar. We, as a nation, have adopted the USDA food pyramid, which results in a high-carbohydrate, low-fat diet. But it seems obvious that this diet plan has failed.

Food is composed of three macronutrients—carbohydrates, protein, and fat. Meats are mostly protein and fat, and plants are mostly carbohydrates. Starches are made up of sugar molecules. All carbohydrates are converted sugar. If you were on a diet of 2,200 calories per day and followed the USDA food pyramid guidelines for 60 percent carbohydrates, your body would have to contend metabolically with two cups of sugar per day. People who lose weight on a diet low in fat and high in carbohydrates will lose muscle. In contrast, people consuming a high-protein, low-carbohydrate diet will lose weight more easily and quickly, usually with little or no loss of muscle.

Cutting out one macronutrient, such as fat, is difficult. The ostensibly reasonable position in the past has been to eat less meat, eggs, and dairy products and replace them with grains, fruits, vegetables, and fat-free snacks. Americans have cut back on protein to eliminate fats. The bad news about this approach is that eating more carbohydrates stimulates the body to store more fat, so many people continue to become fat. Carbohydrates can stimulate profound metabolic hormonal changes. Surprisingly, dietary fat doesn't do much to make people fat.

Figure 16.1 Examples of the five lethal foods.

Eating carbohydrates, even those nonfat foods with carbohydrates, causes a rapid increase in the hormone insulin and a corresponding decrease in its opposing hormone, glucagon. Even complex carbohydrates stimulate that kind of response.

Understanding Insulin

The pancreas releases insulin. Elevated insulin levels can cause monster health problems. The main job of insulin, the master hormone for all metabolism, is to regulate blood sugar levels. Insulin influences every cell in the body. Excess insulin creates havoc in the body that can cause many medical disorders.

People think that cholesterol is completely bad, but if we don't get enough cholesterol our bodies will manufacture it because it is critical to human health. Normally, 20 percent of the body's cholesterol comes from diet, while the body itself produces the other 80 percent, mostly by the liver. Insulin disrupts production of healthy cholesterol. Therefore, we can control only 20 percent of our cholesterol through diet, but by regulating insulin we can control the 80 percent produced by our bodies.

People respond to elevated insulin levels in different ways. Some people deal with it effectively and experience no adverse effects. But 75 percent of our nation's adult population cannot tolerate elevated insulin levels. More teenagers than ever before are having difficulties from excessive levels of insulin in the blood, or hyperinsulinemia.

To counteract hyperinsulinemia (the effects of which could be high blood pressure, high cholesterol, or high triglycerides), many doctors prescribe drugs that affect the ability of the liver to produce cholesterol. But drugs often create other health problems. The good news is that the BFS nutrition plan may help control the body's insulin production without use of drugs.

Genetics play a big factor in the way insulin affects the system. One individual with hyperinsulinemia might have diabetes; another might have heart problems, sleep apnea, or even gout. About 74 percent of Americans are too fat, a statistic that is likely connected to the fact that 75 percent of adults have hyperinsulinemia to one degree or another.

When we eat too many carbohydrates, our insulin level goes up, driving sugar and fat into the fat cells to be stored. One of the jobs of insulin is to prevent stored fat from leaving fat cells. Fat cells are little balloonlike structures whose job is to store calories in the form of fat. These little cells can become smaller or bigger, but if more fat goes in than comes out, excessive weight gain will occur. Obesity is simply the accumulation of too much body fat.

Understanding Glucagon

The pancreas also produces glucagon, the counterregulatory hormone to insulin. Glucagon works opposite the way that insulin does in virtually every way. Glucagon retrieves fat out of the fat cells for energy, and at the same time it blocks entry of fat into the fat cells. Normally there is a balance between the rise and fall of insulin and glucagon. A person with elevated insulin levels, however, will be continually storing fat because glucagon levels cannot keep up. Therefore, those with hyperinsulinemia continually store and accumulate fat. The right food can keep insulin from rising and thus allow glucagon to do its job.

You should thus try to maintain safe levels of triglycerides, blood sugar, cholesterol, and blood pressure. By doing so, you can lose fat and inches while maintaining or increasing your lean muscle tissue.

Shift your thinking. For example, the statement "It's not the potato, it's all the butter and sour cream" is incorrect. Actually, it *is* the potato that is bad, not the butter. In addition, a high-protein, low-carbohydrate diet should not adversely affect your kidneys as long as you start with normal kidney function.

Be On Guard!

Because they contain huge amounts of fat and carbohydrates, the five lethal foods create havoc with glucagon and insulin. You have to be smart and on guard to be successful on this nutrition plan.

Here is what I mean: Let's say that you eat three eggs and some ham for breakfast—the protein-fat time bombs will work *for* you. If you add orange juice and toast (carbohydrates), however, those time bombs will blow up in your face. Listen carefully: If you add carbohydrates to some fat intake, insulin will take that fat right to the fat cells and keep it there. If you don't add the carbohydrates, glucagon will ignore the fat you've just eaten and retrieve your stored fat to burn.

Let's examine a typical dinner—a meat of some kind and a tossed green salad. Good choices, but if you add a potato or fries you are in trouble. The high carbohydrate content of the fries creates a release of insulin that sets off the fat time bomb that was in the meat. Leave the potato alone! If you say, "Well, I used only low-fat margarine on my potato," you just flunked. Begin reading this section again from the beginning. Instead of eating the potato, I like to have low-fat cottage cheese, olives, and even some hard cheese.

Now let's take a favorite fast-food meal—a double cheeseburger, fries, and a cola—and supersize it. The fries, cola, and bun make the fat in the meat and cheese race to your fat cells. Instead, drink water, not colas or other sodas. Have another double cheeseburger instead of the fries. Finally, throw away at least half the buns. Eat. Enjoy. Let glucagon suck the fat out of your fat cells.

Athletes' Role

Let's face it. If you have a tendency to be overfat as a teenager, it won't get any easier as you get older. Believe me, it gets tougher. Now is the time to change your habits and start eating correctly. You, not your parents, will be mostly responsible for the success of this change.

A lean, muscular athlete will perform better than an overfat athlete if all other conditions are equal. The lean athlete will run faster, jump higher, and have more agility. The beauty of this nutrition plan is that you can gain significant strength while you are losing fat. Never call this a diet. Diets in which you count calories and eat mostly carbohydrates will usually make you weaker as you lose weight because you are also losing lean muscle tissue, which is bad for an athlete.

Wrestlers should benefit enormously from the BFS nutrition plan. Too many wrestlers starve themselves on a low-calorie, high-carbohydrate diet. This practice is incredibly bad. If you are a wrestler, the BFS plan should keep you healthy and strong throughout the season while you lose unwanted fat. Just think about it. Your competition probably will continue to make stupid dietary mistakes. Your smart choice will give you a chance to beat an older, more talented, or more experienced opponent.

Eat Like a Tiger

I have studied tigers extensively. They are at the top of their food chain and are magnificent animals. What do they do? The first thing a tiger does in the morning is stretch. Then he digs his claws into the tree and pulls (weight trains). Now he's hungry. He slowly stalks his prey, and when he gets close enough he sprints all out. As he closes in on his kill, he jumps to attack (plyometrics).

The tiger drags his kill back to his lair (more strength exercises and variations). He first eats the stomach and intestine area, where the rich, nutritious plant food of his prey is being digested. So, in a very real sense, the tiger eats vegetables and salads. Then he eats the meat or protein foods. The tiger drinks water from a stream that has minerals. The tiger eats all its food raw so it still contains all its natural digestive enzymes. Because we humans cook much of our food, we destroy those digestive enzymes.

The tiger has only one natural enemy, humans, who are destroying the tiger's natural way of life. Thus, the tiger is facing extinction. Humans have only one natural enemy, the same one that threatens the tiger. Humans have given us the Big Gulp® society that produces clever ads that get us to eat the five lethal foods—sodas, french fries, potato chips, pastries-cookies-cakes-donuts, and candy—in huge quantities. Ten percent of teenage boys drink eight or more sodas per day. The marketing strategies of America's corporate empires are literally killing us. Type 2 diabetes is increasing at the rate of 9 percent a year. We have the fattest kids and athletes in history. We are our own worst enemy.

The solution? All coaches and athletes should eat like and be like the tiger. Whether you're thin, fat, weak, or strong, be like the tiger. Doing so will take you to being your leanest, strongest, most explosive self. The tiger must do everything right to be at the top of the food chain. So must you.

A simple way to make great improvements in your nutrition is to avoid foods that contain processed carbohydrates. The most common are what I call the five lethal foods:

1. Colas or sodas
2. French fries
3. Potato chips
4. Donuts
5. Candy

Having eliminated those products, what do you eat instead? The answer is to go for fish, fowl, lean meats, nuts, eggs, fruits, and vegetables. Limit your intake of processed food and make water your drink of choice, preferably water with essential minerals.

Coaches, see if you can get a deluxe salad bar at your school and have attractive varieties of water available complete with ice and lemons. Remember, the key to success is intensity, consistency, and a great natural diet.

Coaches' Role

The implications of this nutrition plan are enormous for coaches at all levels. Coaches, you can now become nutritional gurus of sorts. Counsel your athletes, students, and community. They'll need your help and encouragement off the court or field, just as much as they need your support on it!

For additional information about proper nutrition, consult these excellent resources:

Heller, Rachael F. 1991. *The carbohydrate addict's diet: The lifelong solution to yo-yo dieting*. New York: Dutton.

Atkins, Robert C. 2002. *Dr. Atkins' new diet revolution*. New York: M. Evans.

Eades, Michael R., and Mary Dan Eades. 1996. *Protein power*. New York: Bantam Books.

Sears, Barry. 1995. *The zone: A dietary road map*. New York: Harper Audio.

Kurt Warner—Setting Goals

Kurt Warner knows persistence pays off.

© Kirby Lee

In 1995 a young man named Kurt was stocking frozen foods in Cedar Rapids, Iowa. Five years later, he became the Super Bowl MVP by leading his St. Louis Rams to a 23-16 Super Bowl victory.

Kurt Warner did not start out as the best. After high school Kurt didn't get to play big-time college football. He earned a scholarship to Northern Iowa but sat on the bench for the first four years. Kurt made the most of his chance during his senior year by leading the Panthers to an NCAA Division I-AA semifinal finish. That achievement earned him a shot to play pro football at Green Bay, but he didn't make the cut.

Kurt persisted and kept practicing at Northern Iowa. He played Arena football and spent a year in the NFL European league. Kurt barely made the Rams' 1999 roster. Trent Green was signed to be the starting quarterback, but Kurt went to Coach Vermeil's office and requested an opportunity to compete for the starting position. During the preseason, Green blew out his knee. The rest is history. In the Super Bowl, the Rams were tied with the Tennessee Titans with only 2:12 left in the game. Kurt gathered his teammates in a huddle and pumped them full of confidence. "Hey, we've got two minutes," said Kurt, looking into their eyes one by one. "We've been able to move the ball up and down the field all day. There's no reason we can't get a field goal to win it." Kurt's prediction wasn't entirely accurate. Instead of working his team down the field, he threw a 73-yard touchdown pass play. Kurt was the 1999 NFL MVP.

"I don't ever sit back and think about the journey," said Kurt. "I just think about all the lessons. There were a lot of good times and a lot of tough times. I'm happy. I'll take it all." Kurt added that if anybody tells you that you can't do something, don't believe it. "With a deep faith in yourself, and the good Lord, everything is possible."

Be an Eleven

Champions are not born but made. Only after a lot of hard work and hard choices does an athlete earn the title *champion*. Think of Mark McGwire and Sammy Sosa as they each smashed Roger Maris's home-run record. Think about track star Marion Jones as she swept across the finish line to win Olympic gold. Those were moments created of endless practice, encouragement, and sacrifice.

Everyone dreams of victory, whether a tough running back or a shy teen trying out for a part in the school play. Talent and the desire to succeed are just the beginning. We know that we should follow some sort of path to get what we want, and we know that we will confront obstacles along the way. What we may not know is where the right path begins or how to prepare ourselves for the obstacles. And if we are unprepared, we may lose courage and get lost on the way.

That's where the Be An Eleven program comes in. To help young people fulfill their potential, our program seeks to inspire them to set worthy goals, both athletic and personal, and then to help them develop action plans to achieve those goals. Along the way, they learn about the importance of making positive choices, keeping their self-respect, and being team players and role models for others. The Be An Eleven program is simply about being a success in all areas of life.

IT ALL BEGAN WITH A NUMBER

The Be An Eleven program grew out of an idea I had years ago while giving clinics. I would have the athletes do a box-squat exhibition to demonstrate how great our intensity can be when our teammates support us. I would pick a junior on a team (if it was football, I'd usually pick a running back). Then I would have him put that much weight on a barbell and ask him to perform as many reps as he could with his teammates cheering him on. The kid would always do a lot more reps than he thought he could.

At first we did these exhibitions primarily with football teams. Many years ago I did one for (the late) Coach Travis Farrar's team at Spring-hill High School in Louisiana. When it came time to do the box-squat exhibition, I picked my athlete, and after several warm-up sets loaded the barbell to 400 pounds and then asked the team, "How many games are there in a football season in Louisiana?" They replied, "14." Then I said, "It's really hard to go 14 games, and this young man here is going to show us how hard it is to go all out for 14 games by doing 14 reps on the box squat with this weight." That number worked fine, and during subsequent exhibitions I would always have the chosen athlete perform 14 reps in the box squat. By the way, the following year the team went to the state championship.

The complications began when we started doing clinics for other sports. In basketball a high school team may play 26 games in a season, and in baseball, 30. So what I came up with was to ask, "On a scale of one to ten, what kind of effort should we give? What do you want to be known for?" Immediately one of the athletes would say, "Ten!" but inevitably someone else would top it by shouting, "Eleven!" at which I would roar back at them, "Eleven? What a great idea! So let's vote on it. On a scale of 1 to 10, how many want to be known as a team that gives a ten? How about an Eleven?" And it would always unanimously be Eleven. That's how we decided that the second of our five power axioms would be "Team must establish a work ethic plan. On a scale of one to ten, our team works at an Eleven pace."

The next step in the evolution of the Be An Eleven program grew out of my concern about all the negative behaviors athletes might engage in that could ruin their lives, such as drinking, doing drugs, and committing felonies. Many years ago I had the idea of doing a seminar called Stand Together, with the idea that if we stand together as athletes and support each other, we can help each other to avoid doing these negative behaviors. So I started doing Stand Together assemblies and started thinking that if we could do those assemblies in the right way, then the entire school would want to stay off drugs, stay off alcohol, and not commit crimes. But it didn't work that way, because I found that no matter how convincing the benefits, about 20 or 30 percent of the students would refuse to make such a commitment. Some people within any group will need some other type of program or assistance.

WHO IS AN ELEVEN?

If you are an Eleven, you are trustworthy and dependable. Elevens are people you can always count on. Elevens are goal oriented and make success happen. They are morally strong. Elevens pull others up spiritually, mentally, and physically. They are pleasant to be around in every situation and among all groups of people. Elevens are loving and respectful to others, especially their family members. Elevens make every effort to be great students. They are leaders and do the right thing all the time, even if criticized. They follow and believe in these three rules for success:

- I am worth my highest goal. I deserve success. I will walk, talk, think, and act like that successful person I want to be.
- I will surround myself with positive people, places, and things. I refuse to associate with any person, place, or thing that creates negativity or mediocrity.
- Nothing, absolutely nothing, will stop me from being an Eleven!

Anyone can be an Eleven! It is simply a matter of attitude. It is not a matter of talent or intelligence but a willingness to try continually to raise your personal bar of excellence. Changing your attitude will change your life. You can guarantee yourself success with the right mental attitude. A sign in the Dallas Cowboy weight room states, "It takes no talent to hustle." Those who give it their all every day are Elevens!

Almost everyone is an Eleven some of the time. However, let's be realistic—no one is an Eleven all the time. The goal is to be an Eleven *more* of the time. For some, this goal might seem overwhelming. But there are literally hundreds of ideas and concepts to help. I believe that everyone can make the big time somewhere.

The BFS Be An Eleven program brings many things to your attention that you might not have known or otherwise thought important. Your job will be to evaluate yourself critically in relation to the ideas presented and then choose your personal destiny.

Getting Started

The first thing you need to know in your quest to become an Eleven is that everyone, regardless of ability, has been blessed with at least one

Kerri Strug–Staying Focused

Kerri Strug's focus and determination won her an Olympic gold metal in the 1996 Olympic games.

Kerri Strug was at the center of perhaps the most memorable team gold-medal win in Olympic history at the 1996 Atlanta Games. She illustrated beautifully all five power axioms for success as she played her song in front of one billion people. I think everyone has seen Kerri's vault a hundred times, but let's review the circumstances. A gold medal was at stake against tough competition. Kerri had to make one good vault, a score of 9.493 or higher, and the United States team would win the gold.

Kerri took off down the runway for her first vault, almost as if she were sprinting along the runway of life. She bounced off the springboard, hit the horse, and did a Yurchenko with one and one-half twists. But something went wrong. Kerri's landing went awry. She heard a crack and a pop in her left ankle. Kerri's injury was so severe that some felt she should forfeit and use the several days before the individual gymnastics events to recuperate and prepare herself for the individual gold medals. But the team had set the goal months earlier: to win the team gold medal.

Kerri Strug faced the defining moment in her life in front of hundreds of millions of people who were to witness an event of uncommon courage. In football, when a player is injured, he calls a time-out and has an unlimited amount of time to get back up. In gymnastics the competitor has only one minute. Kerri decided to go for it. Somehow, she had to sprint down the runway. Somehow, she had to stick her landing.

The crowd was breathless as she set her jaw. Kerri blocked out the pain as she raced down the runway, hit the springboard, reached for the horse, and twisted and turned with acrobatic grace. She stuck her landing and quickly balanced on one leg. As required, she raised her hands to the judges. With the vault completed, Kerri collapsed. Her moment was etched into Olympic history as one of the greatest moments in sport. Kerri said gratefully, "You've been waiting for this all your life. Thank you, God."

The American team claimed victory because of Kerri's brave choice. Kerri kept her eye focused on the glory of winning the team gold medal. The pain was not a problem, it was a challenge. She refused to let her pain become a distraction. She had uncommon focus. Kerri Strug played her song and became an inspiration to millions. Her single moment of courage helped untold numbers of others to play their songs.

gift or talent. Your gifts and talents make you who you are. It is up to you to recognize them and build on them. Elevens strive to distinguish themselves from the average and look for ways to create their own identity. To accomplish this you will need to concentrate on things that take effort. Things that express a positive talent. Things that make you stand out from the average.

In standing out from the average you will hold yourself to the highest possible standards so that you can attain your highest personal destiny. That's not all—your example will inspire and help others to attain their true destiny. How do you set those high standards? You do it by establishing your own value system, learning how to judge what brings the most good into your life and the lives of others. Your value system is personal—you should always have the gift of choice. Like a sculptor, an Eleven chisels away imperfections through awareness and by making good choices.

When You Don't Know What You Want

If you don't know what you want in life, if you don't know what your values are, and if you set your sights low, you are bound to end up where you don't want to be.

One way to help you determine your values is to see how you answer questions about them. The box on page 176 lists 10 questions to get you started. Think carefully about your answers.

Hanging Out in the Right Crowd

The people you associate with, the places you go, and the things you do can either help you or hinder you in accomplishing your dreams. We call these people and things dream keepers or dream stealers. The more you associate yourself with dream keepers, the easier it will be to accomplish your goals and dreams. The more dream stealers you associate with, the more distractions you will face. This section will help you recognize the dream keepers and dream stealers in your life.

■ **People.** There are two kinds of people—those who help you keep your dream alive and those who steal your dream. People sometimes alternate between being dream keepers and dream stealers. An Eleven strives to be a dream keeper more of the time. A dream stealer is some-one who tries to get another person to engage in nonpositive or even negative behavior.

If you have worthy dreams and goals, you must constantly be aware of the dream stealers. For example, a person who says that one drink won't hurt you is a dream stealer. People who are engaged in illegal or gang activities are obvious dream stealers. Those people cannot help you

Being an Eleven requires certain personal standards. Striving to become a true Eleven will be the hardest thing you will ever do. It will take great courage. As you answer the questions, think hard about your answers and how you can improve yourself to become Eleven material.

1. Do you have the right to choose to rob somebody at gunpoint?
2. Can you rob somebody without legal consequences?
3. Do you have the right to wear a shirt that says "F--- You" in a public place?
4. How about if "F--- You" is spelled out?
5. How about wearing that shirt in school?
6. Would you ever park your car in a handicapped space?
7. What if there were 10 handicapped spaces that were all empty?
8. You just finished drinking a can of cola and the nearest garbage can is 100 yards away. What do you do?
9. Your mom tells you to take out the garbage. What do you do and when do you do it?
10. You are with a group and they are taking drugs. What do you do? Same question but with tobacco and alcohol. Same question but with stealing a car, tagging, or vandalizing.

get where you want to go in life. Dream keepers are people who will help you keep your dreams alive and help you achieve your goals.

■ **Places.** We can identify two kinds of places. Some places create a wonderful, positive atmosphere, whereas other places create a negative environment. Elevens who are trying to improve themselves and achieve dreams and goals must be able to tell the difference between dream-keeper places and dream-stealer places. Again, you must choose wisely. A party with lots of drinking and drugs is a dream-stealer place. Being alone in a car in a remote place on a date can be a serious dream-stealer place for both guys and girls. Elevens are aware and never put themselves in places that could steal their dreams.

■ **Things.** Some kinds of things help you keep your dream alive. Other things can steal your dream. Many things can be either dream keepers or dream stealers. A dream-stealer thing will create a negative situation. For example, the Internet can be a wonderful thing or a negative one. The Internet can help you keep your dream alive, or it can be a dream stealer. You will have to decide which it will be for you.

Tagg Bozied—Being Prepared

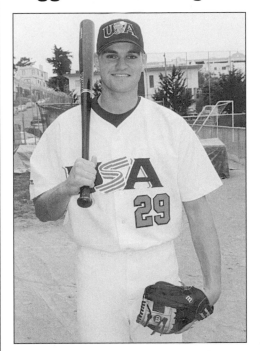

Tagg Bozied knows that being a star is more than just great athletic skill.

Tagg Bozied had a fair year as a freshman baseball player at the University of San Francisco. He was forecast as a probable starter for his sophomore year, but upperclassmen were predicted to be the real stars. Tagg had always been an Eleven, but he stepped it up a notch and became even more focused. He really prepared. Tagg touched the following locker-room sign every day before his workouts, practices, or games: "If you want something that you've never had, you must be willing to do something you've never done."

Tagg had three different mitts—one for each position he played. On each mitt, Tagg wrote the following three words: "Are you prepared?" He was intense and made steady progress every week. Tagg did everything: weights, agility, flexibility, speed work, plyometrics. He ate great, practiced great, and played great. Tagg never had a drop of alcohol in high school, and he stayed away from drugs. In college it was the same story. In fact, when I interviewed Tagg he told me he had not even had a soda in over eight years. Tagg was prepared!

Tagg made the 1999 first-team all-American college baseball team. He made the final cut and was one of the elite top 22 who made the senior national collegiate baseball team. Tagg traveled all over the United States, to Japan, and to several other countries. He led the nation with 30 home runs while hitting .421 in 56 games. Tagg also broke eight single-season records at the University of San Francisco. "I approached the entire season day to day and just tried to do the best I could each day," said Tagg after the season finale. "If I were to look back at the numbers, I guess you could say I was a bit surprised they were that high, but I think I prepared myself for success this year."

CHAPTER

18

Why Steroids Don't Work

Athletic glory, monetary riches, and admiration by the public are among the prizes for athletes who excel at the highest levels. On a smaller scale, young athletes enjoy a rush of pride and self-respect when they best their opponents. Winning is great, and steroids offer the promise to make athletes winners. Given the number of athletes who have tried these illegal substances, the benefits of steroid use must outweigh the risks, right? Wrong! The truth is that the world's best athletes have proved repeatedly that they don't have to take steroids to achieve the highest level of performance.

Most people in our field would say that the statement "Steroids don't work" is absurd. Well, of course steroids work in the short term, but what about the long term? Do they really give an athlete an advantage in a college or pro career? Or can an athlete do better without steroids? Many people define steroids as performance-enhancing drugs. I define them as performance debilitating. Athletes in mainstream high school or collegiate sports can achieve better results through hard, consistent, and smart training. Professional athletes can have longer, more successful careers by not taking steroids. In this chapter I will offer 11 reasons why steroids do not work in the long run for athletes involved in mainstream high school and collegiate sports.

ATHLETES ARE NOT ALL THE SAME

Bodybuilders don't run, jump, or score goals. Power lifters are interested in only three things: the squat, bench, and deadlift. Training programs for athletes, bodybuilders, and power lifters are as different as night and day. People often buy steroids illegally from bodybuilders at gyms. Do steroids work on bodybuilders? Sure they do, and that's the problem. An unsuspecting athlete in a mainstream sport like baseball goes to a gym and takes advice—maybe to take steroids—from a guy who just stands and flexes. Why would he do that? It doesn't make sense.

Power lifters don't stretch for speed and jumping power. They don't work on agility. Do steroids work for them? Again, yes, promoting the same problem. An athlete in a conventional sport like baseball might look at a guy with a 600-pound bench press and figure that this guy can really help him. But that is unlikely to happen. Why? Simple—a baseball player needs to train in a variety of areas a power lifter or a bodybuilder is not familiar with. It's as if a student is playing a complex piece on the piano and getting advice from an advisor to strike one note with one finger repeatedly. The result isn't pretty, and it doesn't get the job done.

STEROIDS EQUAL A ROLLER-COASTER RIDE

Most people get a great high and a great rush of quick strength when they first take steroids, because of the increased testosterone intake. Let's go through an example.

Jim is six feet one and 190 pounds, with a bench-press max of 250 pounds. He then decides to take some steroid pills, but just one dose. In four weeks, he has gained 25 pounds of weight and can bench 290 pounds. Wow! He is on fire. You can't tell him steroids don't work. He has heard about steroids and their dangers, but he thought he would just take one dose and stop. Certainly that couldn't hurt, and he would achieve some fast gains. But by the sixth week, Jim has lost 10 of those 25 pounds and his bench is now 275 pounds. His workouts are all muddled up because he cannot lift the amount of weight called for by his workout plan. His breasts start hurting a little. The injection of a bunch of testosterone into his body caused it to stop producing its own testosterone. Our teen is depressed, so he decides to take another dose. Jim gets another jolt of strength and weight, but this time the effect is not as dramatic. His bodybuilding friend, Dave, advises him to get more sophisticated by changing to a variety of steroids and increasing the dosage. Dave even shows Jim how to inject himself with a needle. To show that he is responsible, Dave tells Jim that he should never share a needle because of the risk of AIDS and all.

Jim is really into the strength and size thing after three months. He neglects his stretching and sprint drills. He spends 12 hours a week in the gym. Overall, his strength and weight gains have been good, but he is never consistent. One day his bench is up, and the other day it is down. His other lower-body lifts have not gone up as dramatically.

Later in the year, Jim enrolls in college as a walk-on. He is scared he might be tested so he quits the juice for a while. He tells the strength coach that he can bench 350 pounds, but when he maxes out for the coach, he can do only 315 pounds. His excuse is that he has a sore shoulder. So Jim goes back to the gym to fix his problem. Dave tells him not to worry and confides that he had started with only 20 milligrams a day but can now handle 500 milligrams with no problem. Steroids are like any drug. The user can become a loser. In this case, are steroids working for Jim as a baseball player? How about as a person? As a student?

GAINS CAN BE MADE HONESTLY

The BFS program has been well thought out and extensively tested. All teens and athletes in their 20s can break eight or more personal records every week—week after week, month after month. There are no ups and downs. Athletes can consistently set records in speed, agility, and jumping. There is absolutely no reason to take steroids. Athletes can make giant gains without them. Unfortunately, many people do not believe that. Recently a semidocumentary TV show called "Flipped" tried to send a message to athletes not to take steroids. At the end of the show, the featured athlete said, "I won't do steroids even though it will be *10 times harder.*" The show's message thus became the opposite of its intent. The steroid myth was perpetuated.

A great strength coach can create positive intensity. An athlete surrounded by teammates in the school weight room who have a common goal can make greater gains than he or she can by working alone in a gym or even with a personal trainer. The same scenario occurs on the practice field or during the game. Teammates working together can create an incredibly intense atmosphere.

Athletes who are persistent and consistent without steroids and know the secret will soon surpass the steroid user, as measured by athletic performance. One final thought on consistency is that many people don't even train when they are on the juice.

UNCONTROLLED AGGRESSIVENESS IS HARMFUL

Many people on steroids enjoy physical confrontations. I suppose gang members might take steroids for that reason. But, you ask, isn't aggressiveness useful in football or at the plate in baseball? That idea holds true only up to a point. An athlete must have a controlled psyche. An athlete who is out of control makes mistakes or can be thrown out of a game. Those circumstances obviously contribute to losing, not winning. A football player has a lot to think about to be successful during a play. On offense it starts with correct alignment and the snap count. On defense it starts with recognizing the formation and certain tendencies. A baseball player with uncontrolled aggressiveness will strike out. Being crazy doesn't cut it.

Hey, I've spent hundreds of hours training with natural intensity. If someone tries to take my position from me or tries to take away my win, he is going to be in for one heck of a fight. I don't need steroids for aggressiveness. I've paid my dues.

MORE THAN ONE WAY TO A FAST RECOVERY

One big selling point of steroids is their supposed ability to allow a longer, harder workout and quicker recovery for the next day's workout. The BFS program easily shoots down that advantage. First, bodybuilders work out much longer in the weight room than athletes do. Bodybuilders usually go six days per week—upper body one day, lower body the next. Athletes need only three days per week in the weight room in the off-season and only two days per week during the in-season. Weight workouts are much shorter, three to four hours per week in the off-season.

As for variation and selection of exercises, the BFS set-rep system includes so many variations that the athlete performs a given routine only once a month. Further, exercises such as the BFS box squat create a tremendous advantage for athletes at all levels. The box squat allows an athlete to recover almost instantly. Any athlete can easily play a game at full throttle or have a quality speed or jump workout the day after a box-squat routine. Athletes hate plateaus. Steroids are appealing because they can jolt an athlete off a plateau, at least the first time. Athletes on the BFS system never experience a plateau because of the set-rep system and the selection of the core lift exercises.

WHY STRESS OVER BEING CAUGHT?

Most users hide their steroid abuse. They go miles from their homes to get their steroids and needles. If they are caught, they could be in heavy-duty trouble. People who sneak around and hide set a bad precedent for themselves. Deceit is an obstacle to winning, a detriment to attaining full potential as an athlete and as a person.

STEROIDS DON'T HELP AGILITY, FLEXIBILITY, OR TECHNIQUE

Training to reach full potential as an athlete is a complex process. Steroid users often place too much importance on size and strength and forget about other areas necessary to winning. During the off-season, an athlete should spend 20 minutes on speed and agility at least twice per week and do a 20-minute plyometric or jump workout at least twice per week. Daily 10-minute flexibility workouts are essential. Athletes who take steroids and think that greater speed and jumping ability will automatically happen are sadly mistaken. Working on the techniques and skills of a sport is vital. Improvement takes time and energy. Athletes who take steroids often fail to appreciate the importance of honing their talents.

Barry Bonds has been accused of taking steroids. Big, strong athletes who produce results, from high school to the pros, are often accused of being on steroids. It goes with the territory. Barry insists that he is not on steroids and says that he looks forward to the upcoming testing in the major leagues. I am confident that Bonds's exceptional batting technique is all his own. Former San Diego Padres superstar Tony Gwynn, now a coach, describes Barry's impressive swing: "Barry sets up the same way every time. Most guys can't do that. What separates Barry is his ability to consistently get his hands and body in optimum position to hit almost any pitch fair. All great hitters get in a position so that your hands can work so your body can work. And that's what Barry Bonds does. Because of his hands, his body goes where it is supposed to go. Barry is always in the proper position. You can't get in on him because he pulls his hands inside the ball. Other guys will hook that kind of pitch foul but Barry takes the knob of the bat and hits it fair."

Barry has a shot at breaking Hank Aaron's record of 755 career home runs. Barry has more going for him than Aaron did as far as knowledge and a support staff. During the off-season, Barry works out five hours a day, probably encompassing all phases of strength and conditioning, including cool-down and recuperative strategies. He reportedly lifts weights so hard that he gets tears in his eyes. Barry has his own nutritionist, chef, and three trainers. Bonds is achieving his goals by training harder and smarter, not by taking steroids.

"STEROIDS ARE A CRUTCH" THEORY

An athlete who looks to steroids to get through a crucial situation has lost the battle. The baseball player who is at the plate with two outs in the bottom of the ninth and is asking himself "Where's my pill?" has become a loser. During critical times, winners create their own intensity and confidence. Winners do not look for external help. They look inside for that something extra.

STRENGTH AND THE DIMINISHING-RETURN THEORY

The stronger an athlete gets, the less important extra strength becomes. For example, it is not as important to add 100 pounds on a bench press that is already at 400 pounds as it is to add 100 pounds on a 300-pound bench. The same concept applies to other core lifts like the parallel squat and power clean. Is a Division I college offensive lineman who benches 550 pounds going to be better than another lineman who can bench only 450 pounds? The answer is no. The same is true of a thrower or a power hitter in baseball. Thinking that Jose Canseco could hit more home runs by having a 500-pound bench press as compared with a 400-pound bench is ridiculous.

After an athlete has attained certain high levels of strength, placing additional stress on the body in an attempt to produce further increases can be counterproductive. Injuries often occur when an athlete tries to reach super strength levels. In throwers, these kinds of gains have proved to be ineffective in throwing farther. In mainstream sports, athletes reach can reach a point of diminishing returns or even a point of no return. Thousands of athletes naturally attain the levels of strength they need for the highest level of performance. Steroids are unnecessary for those who know the secret of training.

The strength levels for college and pro linemen and linebackers and throwers have been established for years. The minimum and maximum levels for bench press are 400 to 500 pounds; for parallel squat, 500 to 600 pounds; for power clean, 300 to 350 pounds. For power hitters in baseball, those levels are absolute maximums and ideally should be a little lower.

The point of no return does not apply in bodybuilding, power-lifting, or Olympic weightlifting. For example, the serious bodybuilder with a 19-inch arm wants a 21-inch arm. He gets that, and he wants a 23-inch arm. Bodybuilders want to keep getting bigger

The massive arm of bodybuilder Gregg Valentino shows that in this sport you can never be too big.

and bigger as long as they have high definition. The point of no return does not exist for some bodybuilders.

A power lifter who works up to a 600-pound bench would be elated to get there but would not be satisfied. If he achieved a 700-pound bench, his next goal would be 800 pounds. The same would be true on his squat and deadlift. The point of no return does not exist for power lifters.

TENDON AND LIGAMENT INJURIES

Information about the effect of steroids on tendons and ligaments has been around for years. If a known steroid user experiences a tendon or ligament injury, steroids are considered a likely cause. Evidence suggests that well-trained athletes who do not use steroids have fewer injuries than steroid users do.

Baseball offers some interesting statistics. Trips to the disabled list increased 32 percent between 1992 and the present. In 2001 the number of shoulder injuries almost doubled. Dr. Charles Yesalis, professor of exercise and sport science at Penn State, says that it would be wrong to attribute this increase to use of anabolic steroids because we don't know what percentage of players have used them. Some players, coaches, and other experts are not as conservative as Dr. Yesalis and are sure that steroids caused all those injuries.

The truth, I believe, can be found by looking at several factors. First, steroid use could indeed have caused some of the increase. A second reason is probably overtraining the shoulder-joint area. Many more baseball players are now lifting weights as compared with 1992. A natural but misguided approach is doing an excessive number of shoulder exercises from a variety of angles in an effort to prevent injuries in that area. I know of one Division I strength coach who probably did more shoulder exercises than anyone and yet was recently fired because of an unusual number of football shoulder injuries.

A third possible reason is lack of flexibility. Most athletes will not stretch on their own. The number-one reason to stretch is to prevent injuries. The trouble is that no athlete believes that he or she will be the one to get hurt. Even when athletes stretch, they frequently use imperfect technique. Softball and baseball players need to stretch for two important reasons. First, stretching correctly can increase the range of motion in the shoulder area. When range of motion increases, a simple law of physics dictates that the athlete will be able to throw harder, faster, and farther. Second, all athletes should stretch for speed and jumping power. If athletes stretch correctly, they should be able to improve their speed significantly, which is obviously important for both offense and defense in baseball and softball. Improved jumping power also means improved explosive power, which should translate into hitting the ball with more power and making more plays on defense.

Baseball players are becoming stronger simply because of the lifting routines that they added to their training programs after 1992. Athletes must stretch hard as they get stronger. Lifting weights need not create tightness. Athletes can easily improve their flexibility by stretching correctly and consistently. Steroids do not improve a player's flexibility in any way and could cause more injuries.

THE BEST DON'T DO STEROIDS!

Most athletes in mainstream sports don't use steroids. The very best players have consistently proved that they don't need illegal drugs to achieve the highest levels of performance. All pro, college, and high school athletes should stand with the legendary players of the past and take pride in their own hard-won strength and conditioning.

AUXILIARY LIFT CHART

Lift	Lift	Lift	Lift	Lift
Sets & Reps	Sets & Reps	Sets & Reps	Sets & Reps	Sets & Reps
Date	Date	Date	Date	Date
Weight	Weight	Weight	Weight	Weight
Sets & Reps	Sets & Reps	Sets & Reps	Sets & Reps	Sets & Reps
Date	Date	Date	Date	Date
Weight	Weight	Weight	Weight	Weight
Sets & Reps	Sets & Reps	Sets & Reps	Sets & Reps	Sets & Reps
Date	Date	Date	Date	Date
Weight	Weight	Weight	Weight	Weight
Sets & Reps	Sets & Reps	Sets & Reps	Sets & Reps	Sets & Reps
Date	Date	Date	Date	Date
Weight	Weight	Weight	Weight	Weight
Sets & Reps	Sets & Reps	Sets & Reps	Sets & Reps	Sets & Reps
Date	Date	Date	Date	Date
Weight	Weight	Weight	Weight	Weight
Sets & Reps	Sets & Reps	Sets & Reps	Sets & Reps	Sets & Reps
Date	Date	Date	Date	Date
Weight	Weight	Weight	Weight	Weight
Sets & Reps	Sets & Reps	Sets & Reps	Sets & Reps	Sets & Reps
Date	Date	Date	Date	Date
Weight	Weight	Weight	Weight	Weight

Only record your major auxiliary lifts, write them in the space at the top then write in the sets, reps, weight and date. Then update this entire page as your weight, time, distance etc. improves. Here are even more Auxiliary and Performance records for you to break. You do not need to record Leg Curls, Leg Extensions, Straight Leg Deadlifts or the Glute Ham Developer.

Vertical Jump		Standing Long Jump		Sit & Reach		BFS Dot Drill		20 Yard Speed		40 Yard Speed	
Date	Height	Date	Length	Date	Inches	Date	Time	Date	Time	Date	Time
Date	Height	Date	Length	Date	Inches	Date	Time	Date	Time	Date	Time
Date	Height	Date	Length	Date	Inches	Date	Time	Date	Time	Date	Time
Date	Height	Date	Length	Date	Inches	Date	Time	Date	Time	Date	Time
Date	Height	Date	Length	Date	Inches	Date	Time	Date	Time	Date	Time
Date	Height	Date	Length	Date	Inches	Date	Time	Date	Time	Date	Time
Date	Height	Date	Length	Date	Inches	Date	Time	Date	Time	Date	Time
Date	Height	Date	Length	Date	Inches	Date	Time	Date	Time	Date	Time

SET RECORDS
BOX SQUAT
OR SQUAT VARIATION

BFS — BIGGER FASTER STRONGER

WEEK 1
3 x 3

3	DATE
3	BODY WEIGHT
3+	EXTRA REPS
	SET TOTAL

3	DATE
3	BODY WEIGHT
3+	EXTRA REPS
	SET TOTAL

3	DATE
3	BODY WEIGHT
3+	EXTRA REPS
	SET TOTAL

3	DATE
3	BODY WEIGHT
3+	EXTRA REPS
	SET TOTAL

3	DATE
3	BODY WEIGHT
3+	EXTRA REPS
	SET TOTAL

3	DATE
3	BODY WEIGHT
3+	EXTRA REPS
	SET TOTAL

3	DATE
3	BODY WEIGHT
3+	EXTRA REPS
	SET TOTAL

3	DATE
3	BODY WEIGHT
3+	EXTRA REPS
	SET TOTAL

WEEK 2
5 x 5

Each block:
5	DATE
5	BODY WEIGHT
5	
5	EXTRA REPS
5+	
	SET TOTAL

(Repeated in two columns for four blocks)

WEEK 3
5-4-3-2-1

Each block:
5	DATE
4	BODY WEIGHT
3	
2	EXTRA REPS
1+	
	SET TOTAL

(Repeated in two columns for four blocks)

WEEK 4
10-8-6

10	DATE
8	BODY WEIGHT
6+	EXTRA REPS
	SET TOTAL

10	DATE
8	BODY WEIGHT
6+	EXTRA REPS
	SET TOTAL

10	DATE
8	BODY WEIGHT
6+	EXTRA REPS
	SET TOTAL

10	DATE
8	BODY WEIGHT
6+	EXTRA REPS
	SET TOTAL

10	DATE
8	BODY WEIGHT
6+	EXTRA REPS
	SET TOTAL

10	DATE
8	BODY WEIGHT
6+	EXTRA REPS
	SET TOTAL

10	DATE
8	BODY WEIGHT
6+	EXTRA REPS
	SET TOTAL

10	DATE
8	BODY WEIGHT
6+	EXTRA REPS
	SET TOTAL

BOX SQUAT OR SQUAT VARIATION REP RECORDS

REP	Establish Records	1st Break	2nd Break	3rd Break	4th Break	5th Break	6th Break	7th Break	8th Break	9th Break	10th Break	11th Break	12th Break	13th Break	14th Break
1	Date / Weight	Date / Weight	Date / Weight	Date / Weight	Date / Weight	Date / Weight	Date / Weight	Date / Weight	Date / Weight	Date / Weight	Date / Weight	Date / Weight	Date / Weight	Date / Weight
2	Date / Weight	Date / Weight	Date / Weight	Date / Weight	Date / Weight	Date / Weight	Date / Weight	Date / Weight	Date / Weight	Date / Weight	Date / Weight	Date / Weight	Date / Weight	Date / Weight
3	Date / Weight	Date / Weight	Date / Weight	Date / Weight	Date / Weight	Date / Weight	Date / Weight	Date / Weight	Date / Weight	Date / Weight	Date / Weight	Date / Weight	Date / Weight	Date / Weight
4	Date / Weight	Date / Weight	Date / Weight	Date / Weight	Date / Weight	Date / Weight	Date / Weight	Date / Weight	Date / Weight	Date / Weight	Date / Weight	Date / Weight	Date / Weight	Date / Weight
5	Date / Weight	Date / Weight	Date / Weight	Date / Weight	Date / Weight	Date / Weight	Date / Weight	Date / Weight	Date / Weight	Date / Weight	Date / Weight	Date / Weight	Date / Weight	Date / Weight
6	Date / Weight	Date / Weight	Date / Weight	Date / Weight	Date / Weight	Date / Weight	Date / Weight	Date / Weight	Date / Weight	Date / Weight	Date / Weight	Date / Weight	Date / Weight	Date / Weight
8	Date / Weight	Date / Weight	Date / Weight	Date / Weight	Date / Weight	Date / Weight	Date / Weight	Date / Weight	Date / Weight	Date / Weight	Date / Weight	Date / Weight	Date / Weight	Date / Weight
10	Date / Weight	Date / Weight	Date / Weight	Date / Weight	Date / Weight	Date / Weight	Date / Weight	Date / Weight	Date / Weight	Date / Weight	Date / Weight	Date / Weight	Date / Weight	Date / Weight

SET RECORDS
TOWEL BENCH
OR BENCH VARIATION

BIGGER FASTER STRONGER — BFS

WEEK 1
3 x 3

3		DATE
3		BODY WEIGHT
3+		EXTRA REPS
		SET TOTAL
3		DATE
3		BODY WEIGHT
3+		EXTRA REPS
		SET TOTAL
3		DATE
3		BODY WEIGHT
3+		EXTRA REPS
		SET TOTAL
3		DATE
3		BODY WEIGHT
3+		EXTRA REPS
		SET TOTAL
3		DATE
3		BODY WEIGHT
3+		EXTRA REPS
		SET TOTAL
3		DATE
3		BODY WEIGHT
3+		EXTRA REPS
		SET TOTAL
3		DATE
3		BODY WEIGHT
3+		EXTRA REPS
		SET TOTAL
3		DATE
3		BODY WEIGHT
3+		EXTRA REPS
		SET TOTAL
3		DATE
3		BODY WEIGHT
3+		EXTRA REPS
		SET TOTAL
3		DATE
3		BODY WEIGHT
3+		EXTRA REPS
		SET TOTAL

WEEK 2
5 x 5

5		DATE
5		BODY WEIGHT
5		
5		EXTRA REPS
5+		
		SET TOTAL
5		DATE
5		BODY WEIGHT
5		
5		EXTRA REPS
5+		
		SET TOTAL
5		DATE
5		BODY WEIGHT
5		
5		EXTRA REPS
5+		
		SET TOTAL
5		DATE
5		BODY WEIGHT
5		
5		EXTRA REPS
5+		
		SET TOTAL
5		DATE
5		BODY WEIGHT
5		
5		EXTRA REPS
5+		
		SET TOTAL
5		DATE
5		BODY WEIGHT
5		
5		EXTRA REPS
5+		
		SET TOTAL
5		DATE
5		BODY WEIGHT
5		
5		EXTRA REPS
5+		
		SET TOTAL
5		DATE
5		BODY WEIGHT
5		
5		EXTRA REPS
5+		
		SET TOTAL
5		DATE
5		BODY WEIGHT
5		
5		EXTRA REPS
5+		
		SET TOTAL
5		DATE
5		BODY WEIGHT
5		
5		EXTRA REPS
5+		
		SET TOTAL

WEEK 3
5-4-3-2-1

5		DATE
4		BODY WEIGHT
3		
2		EXTRA REPS
1+		
		SET TOTAL
5		DATE
4		BODY WEIGHT
3		
2		EXTRA REPS
1+		
		SET TOTAL
5		DATE
4		BODY WEIGHT
3		
2		EXTRA REPS
1+		
		SET TOTAL
5		DATE
4		BODY WEIGHT
3		
2		EXTRA REPS
1+		
		SET TOTAL
5		DATE
4		BODY WEIGHT
3		
2		EXTRA REPS
1+		
		SET TOTAL
5		DATE
4		BODY WEIGHT
3		
2		EXTRA REPS
1+		
		SET TOTAL
5		DATE
4		BODY WEIGHT
3		
2		EXTRA REPS
1+		
		SET TOTAL
5		DATE
4		BODY WEIGHT
3		
2		EXTRA REPS
1+		
		SET TOTAL
5		DATE
4		BODY WEIGHT
3		
2		EXTRA REPS
1+		
		SET TOTAL
5		DATE
4		BODY WEIGHT
3		
2		EXTRA REPS
1+		
		SET TOTAL

WEEK 4
10-8-6

10		DATE
8		BODY WEIGHT
6+		EXTRA REPS
		SET TOTAL
10		DATE
8		BODY WEIGHT
6+		EXTRA REPS
		SET TOTAL
10		DATE
8		BODY WEIGHT
6+		EXTRA REPS
		SET TOTAL
10		DATE
8		BODY WEIGHT
6+		EXTRA REPS
		SET TOTAL
10		DATE
8		BODY WEIGHT
6+		EXTRA REPS
		SET TOTAL
10		DATE
8		BODY WEIGHT
6+		EXTRA REPS
		SET TOTAL
10		DATE
8		BODY WEIGHT
6+		EXTRA REPS
		SET TOTAL
10		DATE
8		BODY WEIGHT
6+		EXTRA REPS
		SET TOTAL
10		DATE
8		BODY WEIGHT
6+		EXTRA REPS
		SET TOTAL
10		DATE
8		BODY WEIGHT
6+		EXTRA REPS
		SET TOTAL

TOWEL BENCH OR BENCH VARIATION REP RECORDS

REP	Establish Records	1st Break	2nd Break	3rd Break	4th Break	5th Break	6th Break	7th Break	8th Break	9th Break	10th Break	11th Break	12th Break	13th Break	14th Break
1	Date / Weight	Date / Weight	Date / Weight	Date / Weight	Date / Weight	Date / Weight	Date / Weight	Date / Weight	Date / Weight	Date / Weight	Date / Weight	Date / Weight	Date / Weight	Date / Weight
2	Date / Weight	Date / Weight	Date / Weight	Date / Weight	Date / Weight	Date / Weight	Date / Weight	Date / Weight	Date / Weight	Date / Weight	Date / Weight	Date / Weight	Date / Weight	Date / Weight
3	Date / Weight	Date / Weight	Date / Weight	Date / Weight	Date / Weight	Date / Weight	Date / Weight	Date / Weight	Date / Weight	Date / Weight	Date / Weight	Date / Weight	Date / Weight	Date / Weight
4	Date / Weight	Date / Weight	Date / Weight	Date / Weight	Date / Weight	Date / Weight	Date / Weight	Date / Weight	Date / Weight	Date / Weight	Date / Weight	Date / Weight	Date / Weight	Date / Weight
5	Date / Weight	Date / Weight	Date / Weight	Date / Weight	Date / Weight	Date / Weight	Date / Weight	Date / Weight	Date / Weight	Date / Weight	Date / Weight	Date / Weight	Date / Weight	Date / Weight
6	Date / Weight	Date / Weight	Date / Weight	Date / Weight	Date / Weight	Date / Weight	Date / Weight	Date / Weight	Date / Weight	Date / Weight	Date / Weight	Date / Weight	Date / Weight	Date / Weight
8	Date / Weight	Date / Weight	Date / Weight	Date / Weight	Date / Weight	Date / Weight	Date / Weight	Date / Weight	Date / Weight	Date / Weight	Date / Weight	Date / Weight	Date / Weight	Date / Weight
10	Date / Weight	Date / Weight	Date / Weight	Date / Weight	Date / Weight	Date / Weight	Date / Weight	Date / Weight	Date / Weight	Date / Weight	Date / Weight	Date / Weight	Date / Weight	Date / Weight

WEEK 1
3 x 3

3	DATE
3	BODY WEIGHT
3+	EXTRA REPS
	SET TOTAL
3	DATE
3	BODY WEIGHT
3+	EXTRA REPS
	SET TOTAL
3	DATE
3	BODY WEIGHT
3+	EXTRA REPS
	SET TOTAL
3	DATE
3	BODY WEIGHT
3+	EXTRA REPS
	SET TOTAL
3	DATE
3	BODY WEIGHT
3+	EXTRA REPS
	SET TOTAL
3	DATE
3	BODY WEIGHT
3+	EXTRA REPS
	SET TOTAL
3	DATE
3	BODY WEIGHT
3+	EXTRA REPS
	SET TOTAL
3	DATE
3	BODY WEIGHT
3+	EXTRA REPS
	SET TOTAL

BFS
BIGGER FASTER STRONGER

SET RECORDS

POWER CLEAN

WEEK 2
5 x 5

5	DATE	5	DATE
5	BODY WEIGHT	5	BODY WEIGHT
5		5	
5	EXTRA REPS	5	EXTRA REPS
5+		5+	
	SET TOTAL		SET TOTAL
5	DATE	5	DATE
5	BODY WEIGHT	5	BODY WEIGHT
5		5	
5	EXTRA REPS	5	EXTRA REPS
5+		5+	
	SET TOTAL		SET TOTAL
5	DATE	5	DATE
5	BODY WEIGHT	5	BODY WEIGHT
5		5	
5	EXTRA REPS	5	EXTRA REPS
5+		5+	
	SET TOTAL		SET TOTAL
5	DATE	5	DATE
5	BODY WEIGHT	5	BODY WEIGHT
5		5	
5	EXTRA REPS	5	EXTRA REPS
5+		5+	
	SET TOTAL		SET TOTAL
5	DATE	5	DATE
5	BODY WEIGHT	5	BODY WEIGHT
5		5	
5	EXTRA REPS	5	EXTRA REPS
5+		5+	
	SET TOTAL		SET TOTAL

WEEK 3
5-4-3-2-1

5	DATE	5	DATE
4	BODY WEIGHT	4	BODY WEIGHT
3		3	
2	EXTRA REPS	2	EXTRA REPS
1+		1+	
	SET TOTAL		SET TOTAL
5	DATE	5	DATE
4	BODY WEIGHT	4	BODY WEIGHT
3		3	
2	EXTRA REPS	2	EXTRA REPS
1+		1+	
	SET TOTAL		SET TOTAL
5	DATE	5	DATE
4	BODY WEIGHT	4	BODY WEIGHT
3		3	
2	EXTRA REPS	2	EXTRA REPS
1+		1+	
	SET TOTAL		SET TOTAL
5	DATE	5	DATE
4	BODY WEIGHT	4	BODY WEIGHT
3		3	
2	EXTRA REPS	2	EXTRA REPS
1+		1+	
	SET TOTAL		SET TOTAL
5	DATE	5	DATE
4	BODY WEIGHT	4	BODY WEIGHT
3		3	
2	EXTRA REPS	2	EXTRA REPS
1+		1+	
	SET TOTAL		SET TOTAL

WEEK 4
4-4-2

4	DATE
4	BODY WEIGHT
2+	EXTRA REPS
	SET TOTAL
4	DATE
4	BODY WEIGHT
2+	EXTRA REPS
	SET TOTAL
4	DATE
4	BODY WEIGHT
2+	EXTRA REPS
	SET TOTAL
4	DATE
4	BODY WEIGHT
2+	EXTRA REPS
	SET TOTAL
4	DATE
4	BODY WEIGHT
2+	EXTRA REPS
	SET TOTAL
4	DATE
4	BODY WEIGHT
2+	EXTRA REPS
	SET TOTAL
4	DATE
4	BODY WEIGHT
2+	EXTRA REPS
	SET TOTAL
4	DATE
4	BODY WEIGHT
2+	EXTRA REPS
	SET TOTAL

THE POWER CLEAN REP RECORDS

REP	Establish Records	1st Break	2nd Break	3rd Break	4th Break	5th Break	6th Break	7th Break	8th Break	9th Break	10th Break	11th Break	12th Break	13th Break	14th Break
1	Date / Weight	Date / Weight	Date / Weight	Date / Weight	Date / Weight	Date / Weight	Date / Weight	Date / Weight	Date / Weight	Date / Weight	Date / Weight	Date / Weight	Date / Weight	Date / Weight	Date / Weight
2	Date / Weight	Date / Weight	Date / Weight	Date / Weight	Date / Weight	Date / Weight	Date / Weight	Date / Weight	Date / Weight	Date / Weight	Date / Weight	Date / Weight	Date / Weight	Date / Weight	Date / Weight
3	Date / Weight	Date / Weight	Date / Weight	Date / Weight	Date / Weight	Date / Weight	Date / Weight	Date / Weight	Date / Weight	Date / Weight	Date / Weight	Date / Weight	Date / Weight	Date / Weight	Date / Weight
4	Date / Weight	Date / Weight	Date / Weight	Date / Weight	Date / Weight	Date / Weight	Date / Weight	Date / Weight	Date / Weight	Date / Weight	Date / Weight	Date / Weight	Date / Weight	Date / Weight	Date / Weight
5	Date / Weight	Date / Weight	Date / Weight	Date / Weight	Date / Weight	Date / Weight	Date / Weight	Date / Weight	Date / Weight	Date / Weight	Date / Weight	Date / Weight	Date / Weight	Date / Weight	Date / Weight

SET RECORDS

HEX BAR
OR DEAD LIFT

BFS — BIGGER FASTER STRONGER

WEEK 1 — 3 x 3

Reps		Field
3		DATE
3		BODY WEIGHT
3+		EXTRA REPS
		SET TOTAL
3		DATE
3		BODY WEIGHT
3+		EXTRA REPS
		SET TOTAL
3		DATE
3		BODY WEIGHT
3+		EXTRA REPS
		SET TOTAL
3		DATE
3		BODY WEIGHT
3+		EXTRA REPS
		SET TOTAL
3		DATE
3		BODY WEIGHT
3+		EXTRA REPS
		SET TOTAL
3		DATE
3		BODY WEIGHT
3+		EXTRA REPS
		SET TOTAL
3		DATE
3		BODY WEIGHT
3+		EXTRA REPS
		SET TOTAL
3		DATE
3		BODY WEIGHT
3+		EXTRA REPS
		SET TOTAL

WEEK 2 — 5 x 5

Each cell block: reps 5, 5, 5, 5, 5+ with DATE / BODY WEIGHT / EXTRA REPS / SET TOTAL

WEEK 3 — 5-4-3-2-1

Each cell block: reps 5, 4, 3, 2, 1+ with DATE / BODY WEIGHT / EXTRA REPS / SET TOTAL

WEEK 4 — 4-4-2

Reps		Field
4		DATE
4		BODY WEIGHT
2+		EXTRA REPS
		SET TOTAL
4		DATE
4		BODY WEIGHT
2+		EXTRA REPS
		SET TOTAL
4		DATE
4		BODY WEIGHT
2+		EXTRA REPS
		SET TOTAL
4		DATE
4		BODY WEIGHT
2+		EXTRA REPS
		SET TOTAL
4		DATE
4		BODY WEIGHT
2+		EXTRA REPS
		SET TOTAL
4		DATE
4		BODY WEIGHT
2+		EXTRA REPS
		SET TOTAL
4		DATE
4		BODY WEIGHT
2+		EXTRA REPS
		SET TOTAL
4		DATE
4		BODY WEIGHT
2+		EXTRA REPS
		SET TOTAL

THE HEX BAR DEADLIFT REP RECORDS

REP	Establish Records	1st Break	2nd Break	3rd Break	4th Break	5th Break	6th Break	7th Break	8th Break	9th Break	10th Break	11th Break	12th Break	13th Break	14th Break
1	Date / Weight	Date / Weight	Date / Weight	Date / Weight	Date / Weight	Date / Weight	Date / Weight	Date / Weight	Date / Weight	Date / Weight	Date / Weight	Date / Weight	Date / Weight	Date / Weight	Date / Weight
2	Date / Weight	Date / Weight	Date / Weight	Date / Weight	Date / Weight	Date / Weight	Date / Weight	Date / Weight	Date / Weight	Date / Weight	Date / Weight	Date / Weight	Date / Weight	Date / Weight	Date / Weight
3	Date / Weight	Date / Weight	Date / Weight	Date / Weight	Date / Weight	Date / Weight	Date / Weight	Date / Weight	Date / Weight	Date / Weight	Date / Weight	Date / Weight	Date / Weight	Date / Weight	Date / Weight
4	Date / Weight	Date / Weight	Date / Weight	Date / Weight	Date / Weight	Date / Weight	Date / Weight	Date / Weight	Date / Weight	Date / Weight	Date / Weight	Date / Weight	Date / Weight	Date / Weight	Date / Weight
5	Date / Weight	Date / Weight	Date / Weight	Date / Weight	Date / Weight	Date / Weight	Date / Weight	Date / Weight	Date / Weight	Date / Weight	Date / Weight	Date / Weight	Date / Weight	Date / Weight	Date / Weight

BFS
BIGGER FASTER STRONGER

WEEK 1
3 x 3

BIGGER FASTER STRONGER

BFS

SET RECORDS
SQUAT

WEEK 4
10-8-6

Week 1 (3x3) column:

3	DATE
3	BODY WEIGHT
3+	EXTRA REPS
	SET TOTAL
3	DATE
3	BODY WEIGHT
3+	EXTRA REPS
	SET TOTAL
3	DATE
3	BODY WEIGHT
3+	EXTRA REPS
	SET TOTAL
3	DATE
3	BODY WEIGHT
3+	EXTRA REPS
	SET TOTAL
3	DATE
3	BODY WEIGHT
3+	EXTRA REPS
	SET TOTAL
3	DATE
3	BODY WEIGHT
3+	EXTRA REPS
	SET TOTAL
3	DATE
3	BODY WEIGHT
3+	EXTRA REPS
	SET TOTAL
3	DATE
3	BODY WEIGHT
3+	EXTRA REPS
	SET TOTAL

WEEK 2
5 x 5

Week 2 (5x5) columns — pairs of blocks:

5	DATE	5	DATE
5	BODY WEIGHT	5	BODY WEIGHT
5		5	
5	EXTRA REPS	5	EXTRA REPS
5+		5+	
	SET TOTAL		SET TOTAL

(repeated blocks: DATE / BODY WEIGHT / EXTRA REPS / SET TOTAL for 5,5,5,5,5+)

WEEK 3
5-4-3-2-1

Week 3 (5-4-3-2-1) columns — pairs of blocks:

5	DATE	5	DATE
4	BODY WEIGHT	4	BODY WEIGHT
3		3	
2	EXTRA REPS	2	EXTRA REPS
1+		1+	
	SET TOTAL		SET TOTAL

Week 4 (10-8-6) column:

10	DATE
8	BODY WEIGHT
6+	EXTRA REPS
	SET TOTAL
10	DATE
8	BODY WEIGHT
6+	EXTRA REPS
	SET TOTAL
10	DATE
8	BODY WEIGHT
6+	EXTRA REPS
	SET TOTAL
10	DATE
8	BODY WEIGHT
6+	EXTRA REPS
	SET TOTAL
10	DATE
8	BODY WEIGHT
6+	EXTRA REPS
	SET TOTAL
10	DATE
8	BODY WEIGHT
6+	EXTRA REPS
	SET TOTAL
10	DATE
8	BODY WEIGHT
6+	EXTRA REPS
	SET TOTAL
10	DATE
8	BODY WEIGHT
6+	EXTRA REPS
	SET TOTAL

SQUAT REP RECORDS

REP	Establish Records	1st Break	2nd Break	3rd Break	4th Break	5th Break	6th Break	7th Break	8th Break	9th Break	10th Break	11th Break	12th Break	13th Break	14th Break
1	Date / Weight	Date / Weight	Date / Weight	Date / Weight	Date / Weight	Date / Weight	Date / Weight	Date / Weight	Date / Weight	Date / Weight	Date / Weight	Date / Weight	Date / Weight	Date / Weight
2	Date / Weight	Date / Weight	Date / Weight	Date / Weight	Date / Weight	Date / Weight	Date / Weight	Date / Weight	Date / Weight	Date / Weight	Date / Weight	Date / Weight	Date / Weight	Date / Weight
3	Date / Weight	Date / Weight	Date / Weight	Date / Weight	Date / Weight	Date / Weight	Date / Weight	Date / Weight	Date / Weight	Date / Weight	Date / Weight	Date / Weight	Date / Weight	Date / Weight
4	Date / Weight	Date / Weight	Date / Weight	Date / Weight	Date / Weight	Date / Weight	Date / Weight	Date / Weight	Date / Weight	Date / Weight	Date / Weight	Date / Weight	Date / Weight	Date / Weight
5	Date / Weight	Date / Weight	Date / Weight	Date / Weight	Date / Weight	Date / Weight	Date / Weight	Date / Weight	Date / Weight	Date / Weight	Date / Weight	Date / Weight	Date / Weight	Date / Weight
6	Date / Weight	Date / Weight	Date / Weight	Date / Weight	Date / Weight	Date / Weight	Date / Weight	Date / Weight	Date / Weight	Date / Weight	Date / Weight	Date / Weight	Date / Weight	Date / Weight
8	Date / Weight	Date / Weight	Date / Weight	Date / Weight	Date / Weight	Date / Weight	Date / Weight	Date / Weight	Date / Weight	Date / Weight	Date / Weight	Date / Weight	Date / Weight	Date / Weight
10	Date / Weight	Date / Weight	Date / Weight	Date / Weight	Date / Weight	Date / Weight	Date / Weight	Date / Weight	Date / Weight	Date / Weight	Date / Weight	Date / Weight	Date / Weight	Date / Weight

BIGGER FASTER STRONGER
BFS

SET RECORDS

BENCH

WEEK 1 (3 x 3)

3		DATE
3		BODY WEIGHT
3+		EXTRA REPS
		SET TOTAL

3		DATE
3		BODY WEIGHT
3+		EXTRA REPS
		SET TOTAL

3		DATE
3		BODY WEIGHT
3+		EXTRA REPS
		SET TOTAL

3		DATE
3		BODY WEIGHT
3+		EXTRA REPS
		SET TOTAL

3		DATE
3		BODY WEIGHT
3+		EXTRA REPS
		SET TOTAL

3		DATE
3		BODY WEIGHT
3+		EXTRA REPS
		SET TOTAL

3		DATE
3		BODY WEIGHT
3+		EXTRA REPS
		SET TOTAL

3		DATE
3		BODY WEIGHT
3+		EXTRA REPS
		SET TOTAL

WEEK 2 (5 x 5)

Repeated blocks:

5		DATE	5	DATE
5		BODY WEIGHT	5	BODY WEIGHT
5			5	
5		EXTRA REPS	5	EXTRA REPS
5+			5+	
		SET TOTAL		SET TOTAL

(four such paired blocks)

WEEK 3 (5-4-3-2-1)

5		DATE	5	DATE
4		BODY WEIGHT	4	BODY WEIGHT
3			3	
2		EXTRA REPS	2	EXTRA REPS
1+			1+	
		SET TOTAL		SET TOTAL

(four such paired blocks)

WEEK 4 (10-8-6)

10		DATE
8		BODY WEIGHT
6+		EXTRA REPS
		SET TOTAL

10		DATE
8		BODY WEIGHT
6+		EXTRA REPS
		SET TOTAL

10		DATE
8		BODY WEIGHT
6+		EXTRA REPS
		SET TOTAL

10		DATE
8		BODY WEIGHT
6+		EXTRA REPS
		SET TOTAL

10		DATE
8		BODY WEIGHT
6+		EXTRA REPS
		SET TOTAL

10		DATE
8		BODY WEIGHT
6+		EXTRA REPS
		SET TOTAL

10		DATE
8		BODY WEIGHT
6+		EXTRA REPS
		SET TOTAL

BENCH REP RECORDS

REP	Establish Records	1st Break	2nd Break	3rd Break	4th Break	5th Break	6th Break	7th Break	8th Break	9th Break	10th Break	11th Break	12th Break	13th Break	14th Break
1	Date / Weight	Date / Weight	Date / Weight	Date / Weight	Date / Weight	Date / Weight	Date / Weight	Date / Weight	Date / Weight	Date / Weight	Date / Weight	Date / Weight	Date / Weight	Date / Weight	Date / Weight
2	Date / Weight	Date / Weight	Date / Weight	Date / Weight	Date / Weight	Date / Weight	Date / Weight	Date / Weight	Date / Weight	Date / Weight	Date / Weight	Date / Weight	Date / Weight	Date / Weight	Date / Weight
3	Date / Weight	Date / Weight	Date / Weight	Date / Weight	Date / Weight	Date / Weight	Date / Weight	Date / Weight	Date / Weight	Date / Weight	Date / Weight	Date / Weight	Date / Weight	Date / Weight	Date / Weight
4	Date / Weight	Date / Weight	Date / Weight	Date / Weight	Date / Weight	Date / Weight	Date / Weight	Date / Weight	Date / Weight	Date / Weight	Date / Weight	Date / Weight	Date / Weight	Date / Weight	Date / Weight
5	Date / Weight	Date / Weight	Date / Weight	Date / Weight	Date / Weight	Date / Weight	Date / Weight	Date / Weight	Date / Weight	Date / Weight	Date / Weight	Date / Weight	Date / Weight	Date / Weight	Date / Weight
6	Date / Weight	Date / Weight	Date / Weight	Date / Weight	Date / Weight	Date / Weight	Date / Weight	Date / Weight	Date / Weight	Date / Weight	Date / Weight	Date / Weight	Date / Weight	Date / Weight	Date / Weight
8	Date / Weight	Date / Weight	Date / Weight	Date / Weight	Date / Weight	Date / Weight	Date / Weight	Date / Weight	Date / Weight	Date / Weight	Date / Weight	Date / Weight	Date / Weight	Date / Weight	Date / Weight
10	Date / Weight	Date / Weight	Date / Weight	Date / Weight	Date / Weight	Date / Weight	Date / Weight	Date / Weight	Date / Weight	Date / Weight	Date / Weight	Date / Weight	Date / Weight	Date / Weight	Date / Weight

GOAL RECORD CHART

To use the goal setting chart properly, follow these instructions. <u>Do not record any goals until you have gone through the entire program for 3 to 4 weeks</u>. After this amount of time, you will know exactly what your real starting performance is in all the events. The next step is to decide what you want to achieve in each event at the end of the year, record these figures under "year end goal". You then will set goals one month at a time accomplishing these monthly goals until you achieve your year end goals. Remember to record what you actually achieve after each month to help you to stay on track. Good Luck and remember the "Sky's the Limit."

EXERCISE	MONTH 1	MONTH 2	MONTH 3	MONTH 4	MONTH 5	MONTH 6	MONTH 7	MONTH 8	MONTH 9	MONTH 10	MONTH 11	YEAR END GOAL
BENCH	GOAL	GOAL	GOAL	GOAL	GOAL	GOAL	GOAL	GOAL	GOAL	GOAL	GOAL	GOAL
	ACTUAL	ACTUAL	ACTUAL	ACTUAL	ACTUAL	ACTUAL	ACTUAL	ACTUAL	ACTUAL	ACTUAL	ACTUAL	ACTUAL
SQUAT	GOAL	GOAL	GOAL	GOAL	GOAL	GOAL	GOAL	GOAL	GOAL	GOAL	GOAL	GOAL
	ACTUAL	ACTUAL	ACTUAL	ACTUAL	ACTUAL	ACTUAL	ACTUAL	ACTUAL	ACTUAL	ACTUAL	ACTUAL	ACTUAL
CLEAN	GOAL	GOAL	GOAL	GOAL	GOAL	GOAL	GOAL	GOAL	GOAL	GOAL	GOAL	GOAL
	ACTUAL	ACTUAL	ACTUAL	ACTUAL	ACTUAL	ACTUAL	ACTUAL	ACTUAL	ACTUAL	ACTUAL	ACTUAL	ACTUAL
HEX BAR DEAD LIFT	GOAL	GOAL	GOAL	GOAL	GOAL	GOAL	GOAL	GOAL	GOAL	GOAL	GOAL	GOAL
	ACTUAL	ACTUAL	ACTUAL	ACTUAL	ACTUAL	ACTUAL	ACTUAL	ACTUAL	ACTUAL	ACTUAL	ACTUAL	ACTUAL
DEAD LIFT	GOAL	GOAL	GOAL	GOAL	GOAL	GOAL	GOAL	GOAL	GOAL	GOAL	GOAL	GOAL
	ACTUAL	ACTUAL	ACTUAL	ACTUAL	ACTUAL	ACTUAL	ACTUAL	ACTUAL	ACTUAL	ACTUAL	ACTUAL	ACTUAL
40 YARD DASH	GOAL	GOAL	GOAL	GOAL	GOAL	GOAL	GOAL	GOAL	GOAL	GOAL	GOAL	GOAL
	ACTUAL	ACTUAL	ACTUAL	ACTUAL	ACTUAL	ACTUAL	ACTUAL	ACTUAL	ACTUAL	ACTUAL	ACTUAL	ACTUAL
20 YARD DASH	GOAL	GOAL	GOAL	GOAL	GOAL	GOAL	GOAL	GOAL	GOAL	GOAL	GOAL	GOAL
	ACTUAL	ACTUAL	ACTUAL	ACTUAL	ACTUAL	ACTUAL	ACTUAL	ACTUAL	ACTUAL	ACTUAL	ACTUAL	ACTUAL
DOT DRILL (AGILITY EVENT)	GOAL	GOAL	GOAL	GOAL	GOAL	GOAL	GOAL	GOAL	GOAL	GOAL	GOAL	GOAL
	ACTUAL	ACTUAL	ACTUAL	ACTUAL	ACTUAL	ACTUAL	ACTUAL	ACTUAL	ACTUAL	ACTUAL	ACTUAL	ACTUAL
STANDING LONG JUMP	GOAL	GOAL	GOAL	GOAL	GOAL	GOAL	GOAL	GOAL	GOAL	GOAL	GOAL	GOAL
	ACTUAL	ACTUAL	ACTUAL	ACTUAL	ACTUAL	ACTUAL	ACTUAL	ACTUAL	ACTUAL	ACTUAL	ACTUAL	ACTUAL
VERTICAL JUMP	GOAL	GOAL	GOAL	GOAL	GOAL	GOAL	GOAL	GOAL	GOAL	GOAL	GOAL	GOAL
	ACTUAL	ACTUAL	ACTUAL	ACTUAL	ACTUAL	ACTUAL	ACTUAL	ACTUAL	ACTUAL	ACTUAL	ACTUAL	ACTUAL

BIBLIOGRAPHY

Adams, Kent, O'Shea, John P., O'Shea, Katie L., Climstein, Mike. 1992. The effect of six weeks of squat, plyometric and squat-plyometric training on power production. *The Journal of Strength and Conditioning Research.* Vol.1, No.1, pp.36-41.

Shillington, Mark. 2002. Strength and Conditioning Coach. Vol.9, No.3.

Siff, Mel. 1998. *Facts and Fallacies of Fitness* (2e).

Zatsiorsky, Vladimir. 1995. *Science and Practice of Strength Training.* Champaign, IL: Human Kinetics.

Note: The italicized *f* and *t* following page numbers refer to figures and tables, respectively.

Index

Index

Dr. Greg Shepard is one of the most influential strength coaches in the United States. He has coached three Division I football schools and was a strength and conditioning consultant for the Utah Jazz from 1981 to 1997. He was selected as the Football Coach of the Year in Utah in 1975, and over the past 25 years he has given more than 500 seminars to coaches and athletes in all 50 states. More than 9,000 high schools have implemented Dr. Shepard's Bigger Faster Stronger (BFS) program, and of these schools, more than 300 have won state championships in football after having had BFS clinics.

Dr. Shepard received his doctorate in physical education from Brigham Young University. In 1977 he became the president of BFS, an exercise equipment manufacturing facility in Salt Lake City, Utah. For the past 25 years Dr. Shepard has been the publisher of *Bigger Faster Stronger*, a sports conditioning magazine that is distributed to every high school, college, and professional football team in the country. He is also the author of 4 books and 23 videos on sport conditioning. Dr. Shepard is married with four children and currently lives in Provo, Utah.

Develop Successful Athletes!

Fuel for Young Athletes provides essential dietary information for optimal physical development and sport participation for teenagers from the middle school through high school years. It contains food plans to tackle the demands of specific sports, and recipe and snack ideas that will appeal to this age group and will power their performance on the playing fields or courts.

200 pages • 0-7360-4652-6

Creative Coaching is a strategic handbook for addressing the challenges of coaching modern athletes and maximizing their sport performance. Written by one of the top coaching consultants in the U.S., the book presents innovative approaches with proven payoffs.

232 pages • 0-7360-3327-0

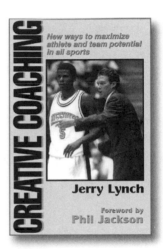

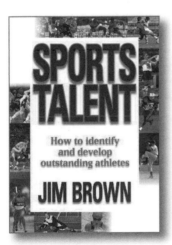

Sports Talent has a wealth of input from top experts and coaches who address key issues, sport-specific evaluations, and training development methods in 13 different sports for boys and girls. This easy-to-follow guide will provide much needed insight on how to develop talented athletes to their fullest potential.

312 pages • 0-7360-3390-4

For a complete description or to order

call 800-747-4457

CANADA: 800-465-7301
AUSTRALIA: 08 8277 1555
NEW ZEALAND: 0064 9 448 1207
EUROPE: +44 (0) 113 255 5665
WEB SITE: www.HumanKinetics.com

HUMAN KINETICS
The Premier Publisher for Sports & Fitness
P.O. Box 5076, Champaign, IL 61825-5076